HUMILIATION

COLLECTION MANAGEMENT

HUMILIATION

Wayne Koestenbaum

BIG IDEAS/SMALL BOOKS

PICADOR

New York

www.picadorusa.com

Picador® is a U.S. registered trademark and is used by St. Martin's Press under license from Pan Books Limited.

For information on Picador Reading Group Guides, please contact Picador.

E-mail: readinggroupguides@picadorusa.com

An extension of this copyright follows page 185.

Library of Congress Cataloging-in-Publication Data

Koestenbaum, Wayne.
    Humiliation / Wayne Koestenbaum.
        p.   cm.
    ISBN 978-0-312-42922-5
    1. Humiliation. 2. Shame. I. Title.
    BF575.H85K64 2011
    152.4'4—dc21
                        2011012702

First Edition: August 2011

10 9 8 7 6 5 4 3 2 1

152.44

CONTENTS

FUGUE #1

STRIP SEARCH

1.

Recently in New York City an arrested man was strip-searched—standard procedure—on Rikers Island. The arraigned man said, "I was put into a cage and told to take off my clothes." He was ordered—according to *The New York Times*—"to squat and spread his buttocks." The accused, who'd been arrested for possession of marijuana, described the strip search as "horrifying": "Being a grown man, I was humiliated."

2.

"Humiliation" means "to be made humble." To be made human? "Human" and "humiliation" do not share an etymological root, but even in Latin the two words—*humanus* and *humiliatio*—suggestively share a prefix.

3.

Repeatedly I watch clips of Liza Minnelli on YouTube. I want to see her humiliation. And I want to see her survive the grisly experience and turn it into glory.

4.

Being humiliated is an experience, I presume, that you don't want—unless you're a masochist. And then your humiliation isn't dire. It's pleasure. Humiliation, if passed through the masochistic centrifuge, becomes joy, or uplift—all emotional dissonances resolved.

5.

An oft-repeated legend: the writer Colette was locked in her room by her husband, Willy, so that she'd be forced to produce her Claudine novels. Need I humiliate myself to write this book?

6.

Michael Jackson's father beat him; MGM fed "uppers" to Judy Garland. The performer must be coerced or brutalized to perform. "Beat It" and "Over the Rainbow" reverse the humiliation, or continue it.

7.

Performers spawn performers, an intergenerational saga of distress. Liza (in the eyes of a shame-hungry public) is humiliated by inability to reach her mother's pinnacle, or by inability to reach her own former pinnacle. Past triumphs rise up to humiliate the present self.

8.

To prove that humiliation exists, we don't need to hear from witnesses. Everyone has been humiliated, although the texture of each person's experience differs—like Tolstoy's unhappy families, each unhappy in its own way.

9.

Imagine a society in which humiliation is essential—as a rite of passage, as a passport to decency and civilization, as a necessary shedding of hubris.

10.

Any writer's humiliation I take personally. "I don't want poets to be humiliated," writes poet Ruth Padel, about the smear campaign against rival Derek Walcott, accused of sexual harassment. But then the press revealed that she'd helped spread the bad word about Walcott, and she, in turn, was disgraced. Retelling this story, I wince: I'm tainted by the news I leak.

11.

According to feminist Mary Daly (quoted in Adrienne Rich's *Of Woman Born*), "Many would see abortion as a humiliating procedure." Many would see insemination as a humiliating procedure. Many would see death as a humiliating procedure. Many would see literacy as a humiliating procedure.

12.

I approach this vast subject from a limited angle—the angle of fatigue. I am tired, as any human must be, after a life spent avoiding humiliation and yet standing near its flame, enjoying the sparks, the heat, the paradoxical illumination.

13.

Not merely because I am tired, but because this subject, humiliation, is monstrous, and because it erodes the voice that tries to lay siege to its complexities, I will resign myself, in the fugues that follow, to setting forth an openended series of paradoxes and juxtapositions. (I call these excursions "fugues" not only because I want the rhetorical license offered by invoking counterpoint but because a "fugue state" is a mentally unbalanced condition of dissociated wandering away from one's own identity.) Some of my fugal juxtapositions are literal and logical, while others are figurative, meant merely to suggest the presence of undercurrents, sympathies, resonances shared between essentially *unlike* experiences. If there is any reward to be found in this exercise of juxtaposing contraries to detect the occasional gleam of likeness, that dividend lies in the apprehension of a singular prey: the detection of a whimpering beast inside each of us, a beast whose cries are micropitches, too faint for regular notation.

14.

When I see a public figure humiliated, I feel empathy. I imagine: *that martyr could be me.* Even if the public figure did something wrong, I empathize. Even if Michael Jackson slept with children. Even if Roman Polanski raped a thirteen-year-old. When I see the famous figure brought to trial, even if only trial-by-media, *especially if the crime is sexual,* I'm seized by horror and fascination, by pity, by terror: here again, as if at the Acropolis or the Roman Colosseum, I see the dramatic onset of a familiar scene, an unveiling, a goring, a staining, a stripping away of privilege.

15.

Speaking, I'm on display—a pornographic exhibit. I'm a centerfold, my legs spread. If someone sees my nude photo on the Internet, then I'm humiliated, or else that Web trawler, finding my photo, is humiliated on my behalf.

16.

When I found a student's nude photo on the Web, and when I jerked off to that photo (I could be making up this fact), I worried that I'd humiliated him. Or perhaps I'm humiliating the student by telling you this story now. Lest you wish to prosecute me for my fantasies, please know that the student was in his late twenties and was advertising his sexual services. In the photo, he smiled with what seemed authentic gladness.

17.

After a fight, an eighteen-year-old boy in Florida sends a nude photograph of his underage girlfriend (she is sixteen) to "dozens of people, including her parents," according to *The New York Times*, whose pages I cruise for humiliation. By clipping the news stories, I become a guilty party.

18.

Sexuality, in any of its guises and positions, is potentially humiliating. At least the Transcendental feminist Marga-ret Fuller thought so. Elizabeth Hardwick, who wrote eloquently about seduced women, quotes a telling passage: when Fuller's boyfriend or husband forced her to have sex, she experienced "what was to every worthy and womanly feeling so humiliating." And in Harriet Jacobs's now-canonical *Incidents in the Life of a Slave Girl: Written by Herself,* the writer reserves the word "humiliation" for instances of *sexual* degradation. The fact of being enslaved she doesn't refer to as humiliating. What is humiliating is the sexual body itself, its humors and swellings, its pulsations and emissions. Theorist Julia Kristeva uses the word "abject" to describe this fetid, wet, organ-centered process.

19.

The Marquis de Sade piles up humiliations, and I aim to do the same. The pleasure some of us get from watching TV or appearing on TV, or the pleasure some of us get from porn, or the pleasure some of us get from disliking sexual criminals—the pleasure (or call it an emotion more complex than pleasure) some of us get from spectacles of all kinds is connected to what transpires in the torture room.

20.

The Abu Ghraib photos made torture topical. A U.S. Army reservist—Lynndie England, joined by leering peers—posed beside a "pyramid" of stripped Iraqi men; humiliating them, she turned herself into an internationally maligned object. Her pose—her apparent gladness—seemed to epitomize the sportive nature of U.S.-style humiliation: we're cheerful decimators. (Whenever I bring up torture, a depressed sense of never being able to sound the depths of this dismal subject assails me.)

21.

Why do people want to appear on reality TV shows in humiliating guises and situations? (Displaying a fat body. Singing badly. Stuttering.) You'd think they'd want to hide their humiliation rather than parade it. Display, evidently, is considered healing—steam released, trauma canceled. The psychoanalytic word "abreactive" describes what we achieve by undergoing humiliation or by not making a secret of it. Abreaction, according to my trusty *Oxford American Dictionary*, is "the expression and consequent release of a previously repressed emotion, achieved through reliving the experience that caused it." Writing is abreactive—I release the emotion of humiliation by replaying it.

22.

To avoid humiliation, which is the feared and inevitable outcome of most writing, especially if it knows itself to be writing, I need to speak from a position of wisdom, omniscience, authority. I can't merely pile up the sordid, nude examples. I acquire mastery by stating an argument. Here are its splayed elements.

23.

Humiliation involves a triangle: (1) the victim, (2) the abuser, and (3) the witness. The humiliated person may also behold her own degradation, or may imagine someone else, in the future, watching it or hearing about it.

The scene's horror—its energy, its electricity—involves the presence of *three*. An infernal waltz.

24.

Humiliation, a topsy-turvy regime, involves a reversal: from top to bottom, from high to low, from exalted to degraded, from secure to insecure. The reversal happens quickly. Someone must be there to watch it happen, and to carry the news elsewhere.

25.

Humiliation involves physical process: fluids, solids, organs, cavities, orifices, outpourings, ingestions, excrescences, spillages. Humiliation demands a soiling. Even if the ordeal is merely mental, the body itself gets dragged into the mess.

26.

Humiliation involves the classic trio of social markers: gender, race, class. Humiliation depends on what you look like, what you sound like, how much money you make, how you walk, how you smell, where you put your garbage. Humiliation hits us where we live, on the confusing, inexorably determining grid of blackness, whiteness, maleness, femaleness, in-betweenness. If we dwell in limbo, in transition, that homeless location, too, is humiliating.

27.

Humiliation has its rewards. Among them: the privilege of being seen as exemplary. The pleasure of being a spectacle. The perk of visibility, of becoming legible.

28.

Another reward: identification with the downtrodden. If you humiliate me, I enter a new community, a fellowship—across history—of sufferers and outcasts. Jesus, once a Jew, is more than a bit player in this bloody drama.

29.

The person doing the humiliation—aggressor, tyrant, bully, monolith, petty soldier, priest, poet—is humiliated by the act. (Even Jesus knew how to dish it out: he told Mary, Mother of God, "Woman, what have I to do with thee?") And so the humiliator (the instigator) is besmirched, reflexively, by the act—if only in the eyes of the victim and the witness.

30.

Humiliation comes with its own proscenium—a ready-made orchestra pit, curtain, audience, lights, ticket booth. Humiliation contains an entire theatrical apparatus, even if only in the minds of the soiled parties (tyrant, victim, witness). Or in God's mind. God, we assume, sees every humiliation; He may not create or approve of the humiliation, but He sees it happening. Humiliation is a frame for making sense of reality. Such a frame we might call an "optic"—a way of seeing.

31.

Humiliation is external, though it registers internally. Shame, on the other hand, can arise simply internally, without any reference to outside circumstances. Humiliation, I believe, must arise (if only in imagination) from outside. Humiliation is an observable lowering of status and position. One can be humiliated without being ashamed, or even without being sad. Humiliation pertains not merely to internal affect but to external climate, context, scenario. We can say a room is cold, but that does not necessarily mean that the people in the room *feel* cold.

32.

From some points of view, womanliness or femininity is a humiliated quality. Or else "femininity" is something that can be ruined, impeached, reproached, poached upon—a capacity or endowment vulnerable to smear and stain and scar. Similarly, "masculinity," however questionable a property, and however much women also possess it, is something that can be seen as humiliating (it is humiliating to have a penis, it is humiliating not to have a womb) or as something that can be *taken away* by humiliation (a man who is humiliated has less of a penis than he did before the humiliation occurred). In Freudian terms, humiliation is a castration. A sweet thing gets swiped, stolen—and what remains of "me" is a mockery.

33.

Humiliation is a process of evacuation or depletion. The Greek word *askesis* nobly (if obliquely) implies this rigorous exercise of winnowing away, this shredding and disappearance. Supposedly, energy (the alias of matter) can't be destroyed. But humiliation represents *the destruction of matter*. Something once present—an intactness, a solidity, a substantiality—turns into tatters. Humiliated, one grows less and less. I succumb to a starvation diet. Or, to make the best of it, I become a hunger artist.

34.

Humiliation, however, is also a process of accretion, of accumulation. Humiliated incidents add up; one grows *more and more* humiliated. Humiliation is a growth, a blooming. Pile up the rottenness. Stacks of it.

35.

Or else (as a combination of the previous two principles) one is eaten away by humiliation, and grows more and more spectral—and yet within oneself, a hard kernel, a nugget, a bit of ore, a deposit (like plaque on teeth) settles. That nugget is humiliation: the particle, the remainder.

36.

"A group of lowlifes at a Tea Party rally," according to *New York Times* columnist Bob Herbert, whom I trust to report the dismal truth of this nation, "taunted and humiliated a man who was sitting on the ground with a sign that said he had Parkinson's disease." Debilitating illness shatters the human body and turns it into a pit stop for the urinating dogs, be they Nazis, lynchers, or paying customers.

37.

Humiliation happens only *in relation*. It is a transitive, interpersonal process. One is humiliated only in other people's minds, according to other people's lights.

38.

The physiology of humiliation is at least metaphorically acidic, related to bile, turmoil, roiling, suppuration. For humiliation's soundtrack, conjure a churning stomach. Dry heaves.

39.

Is there *more* humiliation nowadays? Is it escalating? Although humiliation, as a cultural quality, might have changed, at least in recent memory, I hesitate to make historical arguments, or to spot a trend. It is safer to assume that humiliation is historically a constant, its core always the same, the root experience unchangeably, miserably unitary.

40.

Therefore I can't say, "These days, with reality TV, and in the wake of Abu Ghraib photos and Guantánamo prisoners, there is more humiliation." Wrong. The Middle Ages, or prerevolutionary America, I trust, saw plenty of humiliation. To defend this point I can't subpoena two dead witnesses whose reported torments gave me early inklings of this subject's awful magnitude: Joan of Arc, Tituba of Salem Village.

41.

About this timeless fact of social and psychological life, I simply admit: humiliation colors the way I see the world. Furthermore, humiliation colors the way other humiliation-prone people see the world. Humiliation is a pair of filth-speckled glasses. Can we invent a word ("humiliation-radar," "hum-dar") to describe this tendency, this susceptibility to sensing the humiliation of others, or of fearing one's own future humiliation, or of rehearsing (in memory and imagination) bygone degradations?

42.

And must we demand that an economy of transposition and transcendence turns humiliation into a good, a pleasure, a profit, a positive? Must we insist on alchemizing humiliation?

43.

But are there not certain circumstances where humiliation is not just horror, but is a route, a passageway, toward something else, something tranquilizing?

44.

Theorem: the aftermath of humiliation can be paradoxically relaxing. Tranquilizing, to have undergone humiliation and then emerge on the other side. And so humiliation leads to *the cessation of humiliation*. And this stoppage, this reduction of terror, is experienced as pleasure. "After great pain, a formal feeling comes," Emily Dickinson wrote—words that have given consolation to many sufferers. My mother recited them to me over the phone from the hospital when she was recovering from a stroke. The formal feeling—cessation, pause, interregnum, cease-fire—is the payoff for hours of pillory.

45.

Funny fact: when I google "humiliation," number five on the list of hits is the website www.tinypenishumiliation .net, a convenient site "designed for men and women who are into tiny penis humiliation." Evidently there thrives a subculture of men and women who find "tiny penis humiliation" a satisfying, arousing sport—or an activity worth proselytizing for.

46.

In his 1909 novel *Jakob von Gunten,* the Swiss writer Robert Walser (who specialized in literary miniatures) described the bliss of being small: "How fortunate I am, not to be able to see in myself anything worth respecting and watching! To be small and to stay small." He meant not the bliss of having a tiny penis, but, I think, the bliss of being minor, disqualified, forgotten, ignored—the bliss of being downtrodden. You need to be a connoisseur of mixed blessings to endure downtroddenness with equanimity.

47.

Humiliation is bliss if the experience of largeness or magnitude has become overwhelming and unpleasant and you need relief. When magnitude hurts, humiliation (or demotion) qualifies as remedy. For Shakespeare's querulous King Lear, humiliation provides the bonus pleasure of being exiled on the heath, after his venomous daughters kick him out of their castles; at last, after kingship's ordeal, he can enjoy the aftermath balm of wandering with fellow madmen in the storm. Bliss, to be disqualified from power! (Bliss? Perhaps not. But at least Lear relaxes, and rediscovers language, and redefines the meaning of internal sovereignty.)

48.

Humiliation may provoke activism, uprising. The people whom Frantz Fanon called "the wretched of the earth" can reconceive degradation as prelude to (or catalyst for) revolution. The Rosa Parks Principle: years of humiliation lead to epoch-making revolt. Revolt, however, is not always quiet. Choosing homicidal martyrdom as a response to historical humiliation, I become a suicide bomber.

49.

Humiliation—as experience—resembles a fold. From José Saramago's novel *The Gospel According to Jesus Christ*: "In self-abasement his soul shrinks into itself like a tunic folded three times." (Why three times? Three appears to be the magic number where humiliation or holiness is concerned.) The self-abased soul undergoes an inner contortion. Or perhaps any strong feeling resembles a fold, a doubling-up of psychic tissue and terrain, when the self's forward march halts. Imagine folding a napkin, or folding a piece of pasta dough to make a dumpling. I don't know why I'm convinced that humiliation resembles a fold, but I can't erase this conviction. Through the action of folding, the outer and inner realms change places. Think of a defendant, in a trial, seeing his or her underwear presented as evidence by the prosecutor. An object that should be private and unseen is suddenly visible. An accessory appears *in the wrong place*. My unseen experience has been forcibly ejected—thrust outside. The judge hears my secrets. My inner rottenness lies exposed. My skin has been turned inside out. This fold (the self become a seam) is the structure of revulsion.

50.

Humiliation, an educating experience, breeds identity. In Charlotte Brontë's *Jane Eyre* (a novel that taught me, when I first read it, in seventh grade, to understand that humiliation strengthens character), the heroine's identity is formed from her early experience of being locked as punishment in a red room. Her crime? Reading a book that wasn't her property. Jane's identity as *unlovable outcast* evolves in response to this first humiliation; and I'll hypothesize that, in general, identity germinates from humiliation's soil. (Why am I confident that this is true? Do I know what "identity" is? A molten enterprise, it consists, I suppose, in that bewildering and half-inaudible chorus of inner fantasies and memories that builds the illusory sense of ego.) Humiliation isn't merely the basement of a personality, or the scum pile on the stairway down. Humiliation is the *earlier event* that paves the way for "self" to know it exists.

51.

I presume that as moral individuals we should work toward minimizing humiliation, toward not inflicting it. We should practice an ethics of abstention. Vow: I abstain from deliberately humiliating others. When I find myself involved in this abhorrent practice, I will immediately desist and try to reverse the process and remedy the crime. And yet is a world without humiliation possible? It's disenchanting to write about a horrible situation. About this subject, I can't rhapsodize.

52.

Employment is humiliating. Who hasn't heard—or told—a story about workplace humiliation? My boss is a monster. My employees call me Fatso behind my back: I've read their emails. In the TV show *The Office,* the smarmy boss cheerfully humiliates his staff, and the show is a hit, because any working person wants to reinterpret daily indignities—the pus-filled blister of functioning within a bureaucracy—as farce, a style of theater that, as political catalyst, may be more effective than melodrama.

53.

Writing is a process of turning myself inside out: a regurgitation. I extrude my vulnerable inner lining. I purge. And then I examine the contents—my expulsed interior—and begin the bloody interrogation. I ask whether it is filthy or clean, valuable or deplorable.

54.

Is it humiliating to be a prostitute? (Not always, I'd like to believe.) In a TV interview, Eliot Spitzer's paid companion was forced to describe herself as a "prostitute," though she prefered the word "escort." The person who urged the escort to call herself a prostitute was Diane Sawyer, who, like all good TV hosts, combines sangfroid, sympathy, and sadism. Some of us specialize in visiting unclean places; like Diane Sawyer or Barbara Walters or Larry King or any of my fellow broadcasters, I aim smiling questions at my guest's open wound. The instrument of humiliation—or merely its sheath—is geniality.

55.

Monica Lewinsky, Hillary Clinton, and their ilk—betrayed women, seduced women, wronged wives, traduced mistresses—excite my empathy. By imagining what they feel, or might feel, I learn something about what I already feel, what I, as a human being, was born sensing: that we all live on the edge of humiliation, in danger of being deported to that unkind country. Whether wife or mistress, I know that the scandal-consuming public sees me as degraded. By talking about this feeling, or writing about it, what do I hope to prove? Do I expect to excite myself into a rhetorical froth by invoking examples of humiliated people? Do I want to confess my own perverse pleasure in watching their drama? Do I want to tell stories about my own descents into hell? Are these disasters distinct from yours?

56.

I've often feared that the result (if not the intention) of my writing has been to humiliate its human subjects—singers, stars, artists, intimates. My conscious aim was to celebrate them, but sometimes I've been shocked to discover afterward that my unconscious wish was to humiliate them and thereby to grant myself the humiliated identity of traitor, exposer, ingrate, tattletale, usurper, soul-catcher, reputation-despoiler, thief.

57.

And so a theorem arises, applicable to certain writers, researchers, collectors, information-assemblers: *to study a subject is to humiliate the subject and to humiliate oneself by the process of studying it.*

58.

Contemplating a humiliated subject is a form of religious worship. Simone Weil, the anorexic Jew whose self-lacerating ardors inspired Susan Sontag, and who therefore seems a paradigm of the thinker who sees humiliation as pot of gold at the end of the rainbow, found nourishment in meditating on Christ's wounds. In a 1942 letter, Weil attested, with exultant austerity, "every time I think of the crucifixion of Christ I commit the sin of envy."

59.

In today's mail a brochure from the Smile Train arrives, soliciting a donation. On the envelope: a photo of a child with an excruciating, unrepaired cleft palate. (Excruciating to whom? To the viewer, and, we presume, to the child, whose mouth is evidence of a humiliation that the brochure urges me to redress.) Looking at the photo, I experience shock—a spasm containing guilt, anguish, and desperate, fearful identification: if I don't help that child, I will become that child, or I will have retroactively caused that child's suffering. The same magical logic assails me when I behold someone untouchable, or dirty, or homeless, or vomiting, or crying, or shaking, or bleeding, or undergoing an abject physical ordeal. Watching, I sense, first of all, that person's humiliation, and I'm struck by horrified commiseration. Next, I feel an urge to eject that person from my sight: *get away from me, you vomiting freak*. But then a memory appears (*I, too, was once a vomiting freak*), followed by a presentiment (*if I don't help this vomiting person, then I will become a vomiting person again sometime in the future*). And yet I don't want the vomit to land on me. And what if, at the very moment of beholding the vomiting person, I immediately become identical to the vomiting person, whether through paranoid identification or tender empathy? This afternoon, contrite, I write my first check to the Smile Train, if only so I can tell you that I am writing the check. Simone Weil, from her essay "Human Personality": "The only way into truth is through one's own annihilation; through dwelling a long time in a state of extreme and total humiliation." I am not yet an old hand at Weil's art of contemplating defilement.

60.

Google is an instrument of humiliation. I google a rival to see if I can discover unflattering tidbits. And the very process of googling is humiliating to the rival (in magical form), but also humiliating to me. Any time I exercise the privilege of "googling for the hell of it" I am humiliating myself. Much of what I do on the Internet is humiliating. I'm not alone; the Internet is the highway of humiliation. Its purpose is to humiliate time, to turn information (and the pursuit of information) into humiliation. I'd say the same for much of TV, especially reality TV. Many forms of entertainment harbor this ungenerous wish: to humiliate the audience and to humiliate the performer, all of us lowered into the same (supposedly pleasurable) mosh pit.

61.

The newspaper, too, is humiliating—a viper's den, a circle of hell, alive with lamentations. The victim, a prominent socialite, a chemistry student, a working mother, a drug addict, an accountant, a morbidly obese boy with severe mental disabilities, a jogger, an underpaid au pair, a chauffeur, a hotelier, a diet doctor. Photo of a suspect, with hoodie, with Down's syndrome features, with a face like the young Sean Connery's, with a scar above the lip, with a face like the young Jennifer Jones, with a beard, with surgically augmented lips, with a shaved head and radical fringe tattoos on the skull, with a yarmulke, with a charity-gala coif. The accused killer's shocked family, congregating outside the house. Embarrassed or depleted eyes of the murderer's mother, in the courtroom, after the verdict.

62.

Not as bad as 1777, when Ann Marrow was pilloried at Charing Cross (according to the *Newgate Calendar*, a crime chronicle, otherwise known as *Malefactors' Bloody Register*) for "going in men's clothes and personating a man in marriage." When she was placed in the pillory, "so great was the resentment of the spectators, particularly the female part, that they pelted her to such a degree that she lost the sight of both her eyes."

63.

Pedagogy can't do without humiliation. Elfriede Jelinek's novel *The Piano Teacher*—and the movie version, directed by Michael Haneke and starring Isabelle Huppert—contains multiple humiliations; repeating them here might not be fruitful, so I will abstain from giving a complete list. The worst: Huppert hides broken glass in a piano student's jacket pocket; the pupil, reaching into the pocket, bloodies her hand. That's an extreme case of teacherly sadism; nonetheless, any student, no matter how sane and obliging the teacher, structurally occupies the position of *the object in danger of being sacrificed*. Conservatory pedagogy, even when it trickles down to grammar school sing-alongs, has military aspects: a student trained in classical music—or ballet?—knows the pain of getting it wrong, and acquires a gut knowledge of strict standards. Any attempt to teach how to practice an art—even experimental poetry, or performance art, or conceptual art—can easily humiliate, if the teacher isn't careful.

64.

Freud had some silly ideas, although he had remarkable insight into humiliation, which he considered (in his commentary on Dr. Schreber) to be "to the fore" in causing neurosis, especially "in the case of men." What about women? In the case history of Dora, not the climax of Freud's career as a reliable narrator, he opined, with a preposterousness that might be an antecedent of my own, which I hope you will forgive, and which I invite you to see as an echo of your own foolishness (who among us is not a fool, and, as a fool, liable to be the butt of jokes and pillorying?): "Women take a special pride in the state of their genitals; if these succumb to illnesses which seem likely to prompt distaste or even disgust, women's self-esteem is injured and humiliated to a quite incredible extent."

65.

The word "humiliation" gives me pleasure to repeat. It will function, in the fugues that follow, as an incantation. May its repetition, like a swaying thurible, diffuse an atmosphere of forgiveness and solace in the drafty sanctuary. Every time I use the word, I'm striking a bell; its ping announces the momentary cessation of suffering.

66.

I'm more interested in humiliated men than in humiliated women. When I see a humiliated woman (in literature, in life, on the screen, in a dream), I'm horrified and saddened—or indifferent. When I see a humiliated man (on trial, on the street, in jail, in a hospital), I'm horrified, too, but not necessarily saddened; I feel that his maleness has received a necessary puncture. And yet that collapse of maleness fills me with horror. Correction: I'm interested in humiliated women, too. But the spectacle of a man's humiliation has a special ripeness. I may always be wanting revenge on men. And I may, as a consequence, always feel on the precipice of meriting someone else's vengeful attack. A strip search, buttocks spread.

67.

And now I'm making a terrible mistake. I'm speaking in the fictional voice of someone who relishes the humiliation of others—someone who poses as a connoisseur, sampling and savoring humiliation, collecting memories of it. This isn't true. I turn my face, in horror, away from the humiliation of the teenager who sees, on a cruelty-dishing website called Formspring (according to *The New York Times,* my nearest conduit to the national abyss), that a classmate has anonymously written to her, "Everyone knows you're a slut," or "You're ugly," or "You look stupid when you laugh," or "You're not as hot as u think u are."

68.

If my voice seems to assert that *the other* is humiliated but that I am never humiliated, that's a lie. The reason I'm writing is to silence the deep sea-swell of my humiliated prehistory, a prologue no more unsettling than yours.

69.

An iota of sexual excitement—reparative, compensatory—surrounds the subject of humiliation. By talking about it, I guard against its return. Everybody has cause to identify with Saint Sebastian, whom arrows exalted, if only in hindsight.

70.

To speak *after* humiliation: this is the voice of the survivor, who, according to philosopher Giorgio Agamben, speaks an impossibility. The person who was humiliated—he, or she, can't speak. But I, as the survivor of humiliation, can speak on behalf of that person, now absent, now gone. I speak, in these fugues, as witness and guarantor of the humiliated "I," the one who is necessarily silent. But that statement is too serious, too pontificating. And it's too early in the book to bring up the Holocaust.

FUGUE #2

THE JIM CROW GAZE

1.

The position of witness raises ethical ambiguities that have troubled philosophers and saints and other ordinary mortals for centuries; unable to lay those ambiguities to rest, I moonlight as a humiliation-witnesser, mostly through media accounts, reportage keeping me safely remote from emergency. While eating breakfast, I read, in the newspaper, about women with obstetric fistulas in Tanzania, Ethiopia, Nigeria—women who stink, fester, and leak urine (and sometimes feces) all day long, and who are, as a consequence, shunned by their families, their villages. I try to imagine that despond of humiliation; my imagination fails, but I continue reading. From a Nicholas Kristof article in *The New York Times*, I learn that a girl, raped at twelve years old, delivered a baby at thirteen, and suffered a fistula: "The baby's father was horrified by her smell. He confined her in a faraway hut and removed the door—so that hyenas, attracted by the odor, would tear her apart at night." And of this situation I have what to say? Simply that I feel horror at the thought of the girl's suffering, her approach to the non-human, her consignment—on the part of her master, who'd raped her—to the status of excrement. I want to speak up for her—but also to acknowledge that her situation throbs (as reference point) below experiences that

seem easy and trivial in comparison. I want to acknowledge the not-infrequent willingness of a viewer, a neighbor, a master, a lover, a friend, a host, a commentator, to
treat someone else as garbage. The willingness to *desubjectify* the other person. And the willingness, as if in a
nightmare, to lock the door of civilization against this
outcast, and to hear the ruined beast cry in the cold.

2.

I spent childhood watching my siblings getting punished. In memory, I got punished less frequently than
the others. I wasn't as "bad." Didn't commit as many in-
fractions. And this sensation—watching the other child
humiliated—made an imprint on me, turned me into a
curious spectator, willing to shiver into life and identification at the sight of someone else's ostracization.
Why "shiver"? Because, for me, the moment of watching
someone else's—*or my own*—humiliation produces a
shivering, nearly physiological sensation of inner reversal.
The mind becomes Siberia and Hades, simultaneously:
hot, cold. And the body, too, suddenly must host cli-
mactic opposites. Turned into naught, I feel all the blood
drained from my body; I burn and freeze at the same
time. I associate the hot/cold spasm—burning, freezing—
with the sensation of experiencing humiliation or witnessing someone else's humiliation. Not that I want to
reduce every statement to autobiography—that humiliated genre—or to set up some idiosyncratic physiological equation (a hot/cold shiver equals humiliation). And
yet: I'm writing this book in order to figure out—for my
own life's sake—why humiliation is, for me, an engine, a

catalyst, a cautionary tale, a numinous scene, producing sparks and showers. Although humiliation is unspeakably horrifying, it is also exciting, and I keep wanting to approach it, intellectually, to figure out its temperature and position. Any topic, however distressing, can become an object of intellectual romance. Gradually approach it. Back away. Tentatively return.

3.

Did Michael Jackson's father feel humiliated when Michael confessed to the media that he had been beaten as a child? Why am I trying to figure out who felt humiliated, as if this were a psychology experiment? Instead, I should argue for the worldwide eradication of humiliating situations. Writing, I occupy a humiliated position: the voice on trial. When someone speaks, or writes, that person's voice is held captive by the laws of language, and by the demands of the listener. No wonder that some voices in history have exiled themselves from these expectations, even if it meant that the voice stepped over the edge into incomprehensibility, stink, mud, madness.

4.

Psychiatric patients subjected to electroconvulsive therapy—Antonin Artaud (for good reason he invented the Theater of Cruelty), Sylvia Plath (for good reason she wrote "I eat men like air"): did they experience shock treatment as a humiliation? Electric current raped their mad bodies. A foreign agent entered defenseless flesh; the unwanted voltage—too much, too violent—robbed the body of integrity. I'm not adjudicating the value or toxicity of electroshock—for that verdict, ask a psycho-neurologist. But I'm suggesting that we define humiliation as *the intrusion of an unwanted substance or action upon an undefended body.* The pain of the intrusion—but also its suddenness and incomprehensibility (what substance is entering me?)—constitutes the humiliation. The subject ceases to be a subject and becomes a thing acted upon, the terrain on which a violation occurs. Giorgio Agamben calls the procedure "desubjectification." And he suggests that Auschwitz and other death camps were experiments in desubjectification—attempts to turn human beings into the not-human. The experiment was, from the Nazi point of view, a success.

5.

I can't finish watching Michael Haneke's movie *Funny Games:* too painful, to see the thugs torment the suburbanites. I cringe at Lars von Trier's *Dancer in the Dark:* I don't want to see Björk's character hanged. She's blind, she's a mother, she's helpless. Why must I face this horror? I felt nauseated by watching Björk impersonate a woman going blind and then hanging dead from a rope.

6.

When, in Rainer Werner Fassbinder's movie *Martha,* the husband (played by Karlheinz Böhm) kills his wife's black cat, I decide that the suffering of a helpless animal is impossible to watch. Ditto when the donkey in Robert Bresson's movie *Au hasard Balthazar* gets kicked. Can an animal be humiliated? When I terrorize a spider before killing it, am I frightening the spider or humiliating it? What would I learn from figuring out the difference? Does the mistreated animal have a property of dignity or "face" (gaining face, losing face) whereby humiliation can occur? A friend tells me that his dog, when left alone in the apartment, eats its own feces; a veterinarian, when consulted, said that the dog was suffering from shame. (My friend, hearing the diagnosis, felt a sudden blast of shame, as if he'd been accused of abusing his pet.) I've heard people say that they respond more tearfully to the plight of a suffering animal (a mistreated pet) than a suffering person (a homeless person with edema, swollen calves exposed to the elements).

7.

Listening to my voice, I note no excitement: no rush, no rise. Instead, the anhedonia and anesthesia of the humiliated. Murmuring, numb, I am speaking as if already flattened by an injury from which I can't recover.

8.

A woman in L.A. creates a fake MySpace account "with the identity of a cute teenage boy." And she uses this alias to humiliate a thirteen-year-old girl, who, as a result, commits suicide. Thirteen-year-olds are easily humiliated. Like a thirteen-year-old, I depend on email for compliments, affection, rescue, stimulation, greeting. But, if email brings bad news, or information that casts me in a negative light, then the technology itself becomes (by virtue of its impersonality, its silence, its stealth attack) a poisonous substance. Instant communication mechanisms are especially gifted at spreading humiliation's toxic cloud. Does virtual communication make desubjectification easy? The same could have been said about the telephone or the telegraph. Or the typewriter. For a long time, civilization has been in the business of siphoning the body away from the scene of vocal expression, of interpersonal confrontation. More and more, the industries of communication and entertainment—with their globalizing quest to amuse, stimulate, connect—secretly work to deaden, or desubjectify, the human voice.

9.

A melodramatic story line needs a scene of humiliation because it brings a queasy satisfaction to the spectator. (*At least I'm not being humiliated,* the spectator thinks. Or: *I've had that exact experience. I've been humiliated, too.*) From my canon of melodramatic humiliation scenes, climaxes in which heroines, or heroes, stand frozen and observed, encircled by the gazes of others, gazes that single out the hero, or heroine, as suddenly worthless (the victim becomes a hero, or heroine, precisely because these gazes ratify her as the center of a new cosmos of suffering), I choose this touchstone: in *A Star Is Born,* James Mason (playing the washed-up, alcoholic Norman Maine) slaps Judy Garland's face at the Academy Awards ceremony. Judy (Vicki Lester) has won an Oscar; her drunk husband staggers up to the stage and accidentally wallops her. The audience gasps. Judy reels, recovers, and then gently escorts the lush offstage. We weep: Judy/Vicki, the great star, is humiliated at the moment of her triumph. Her husband made a scene. He intruded his filthy dipsomaniacal orality, his vile system of fluids, into her clean arrangement, her new fiefdom (Hollywood success). And so, we feel that Judy herself—the real Judy—is humiliated by stardom. Why should it matter that stardom contains a necessary undertow of humiliation? We may dupe ourselves into thinking that stardom is a positive attribute, a matter of glory and glamour, rooted in physical attractiveness, and yet, by watching stars, we are always *watching out* for humiliation: absorption in stardom (especially the nonentity niches of Paris Hilton or the Olsen twins or a thousand other figures—self-trashing, media-trashed—beyond my ken) is a disenfranchising exercise in scapegoating the objects that we helplessly love. (Not exactly!)

10.

Just as I recognize what it's like to watch someone else get punished, I recognize what it's like to watch someone else make a scene. Drunk James Mason is behaving badly in public—a style of conduct that the public expected from drugged-out Judy Garland. To behave badly onstage is to humiliate yourself and to humiliate your audience and to humiliate those who brought you forward with the hope that you would perform successfully. I may be misbehaving, but at least I'm not slapping Judy Garland. And why must I mention Judy? That's a quintessentially old-school (pre-Stonewall) "gay" mannerism. Doting on Judy is a way of losing control in public. (And yet, it's never too late in history to bring up Judy and ask to be taken seriously. Judy will last longer than her naysayers.) Before long, we will return to Judy, or to her daughter, and to the realm of starry performance, where amity and emotionality are feigned, concealing a dead zone of nonfeeling; but now we have genuinely somber business to transact. It is time to consider the somberness, or deadness, that appears on the human face when it has ceased to entertain the possibility that another person exists.

11.

I call it "the Jim Crow Gaze." The eyes of a white person, a white supremacist, a bigot, living in a state of apartheid, looking at a black person (please remember that "white" and "black" aren't eternally fixed terms): this intolerant gaze contains coldness, deadness, nonrecognition. This gaze doesn't see a person; it sees a scab, an offense, a spot of absence. Nothing in the face giving a Jim Crow gaze will acknowledge the humanity, likeability, or forgiveability of what it sees. When policemen aimed their fire hoses at high school students in Birmingham, Alabama, or when the National Guard blocked students trying to integrate Central High in Little Rock, Arkansas, policemen's eyes—and the eyes of the white spectators, too, the spitters—erased the children. (Elizabeth Eckford, one of the students, remembered, "I tried to see a friendly face somewhere in the mob—someone who maybe would help. I looked into the face of an old woman and it seemed a kind face, but when I looked at her again, she spat on me.") The bigot-eyes will not modulate into warmth. Such a face—a murderer's, a torturer's, a spitter's—declares itself nonhuman. Have you seen this face, these eyes that will not beckon or relent?

12.

I know where I've seen those eyes—a picture in Kate Millett's *The Basement: Meditations on a Human Sacrifice*, her response to the true story of a family who kidnapped a neighborhood girl (Sylvia Likens) and held her hostage in their house and tortured her to death. The picture I remember is of the arraigned mother, the murder's ringleader, Gertrude Baniszewski—a thin, watchful, white, cruel face, whose eyes seem never to have admitted empathy, whose eyes have overseen a cruel operation: under Gertrude Baniszewski's supervision, her kids write "I am a prostitute and proud of it!" with a sewing needle on the kidnapped girl's stomach and force her into baths of near-boiling water. I read Millett's book more than twenty-five years ago; Gertrude Baniszewski's face remains my archetype of moral imbecility, of living-deadness, of eyes that have refused the human.

13.

Lynndie England's eyes seem sicklied o'er with indifference and ignorance. Lynndie, and other American soldiers, piled up Iraqi prisoners, nude, and played games with them. Lynndie posed, smiling, beside the stacked-up, humiliated prisoners. Another soldier, Charles Graner, the ringleader of the torture, posed beside her—but it is Lynndie's face (because of its youth and innocence? because it is a woman's face?) that shocks my senses. (The question of whether she was merely following orders, and whether, as obedient troops must, she had desensitized herself to adjacent agonies, I will leave to other commentators.) Her smile—its indifference—

announces a capacity to enjoy someone else's humiliation and a refusal to register the injustice's depth. The smile attests to deadness. The Jim Crow gaze doesn't necessarily make a loud noise about its process of ostracizing and humiliating the other. But it gives no quarter. It shuts the door against sympathy. The refusal to melt, to forgive, to vacillate: imagine standing in the presence of someone whose eyes refuse to soften toward you, whose eyes refuse to sympathize or to recognize your humanity. And you are humiliated not just by the physical injuries committed against you, or the deprivations; you are humiliated by the refusal, evident in the aggressor's eyes, to see you as sympathetic, to see you as a worthy, equal subject. These eyes disenfranchise and eject the other from a sanctuary or estate—a birthright—that some people call the kingdom of God.

14.

I want to hit the topic—humiliation—head-on, rather than deflect it by listing instances of humiliation. I could make a long, brutalizing list, but instead I want to stare into Gertrude Baniszewski's face (or into faces like hers, an infinite series, in photographs, in imagination, in historical retrospect)—the face of the humiliator, the one who coldly exacts the other's downfall. The white policeman who holds the hose in Birmingham. The white men, a bunch of them, wearing cowboy hats and standing, somber, righteous, beside Frank Embree's lynched body, July 22, 1899, in Fayette, Missouri. I want to stare into those eyes and touch that nonrecognition, that deadness. I'm curious about the face of the person—the

Nazi? the near-Nazi?—who would spit on me. I may never have encountered those eyes, but I can almost recognize them—the humiliator's eyes, looking at me but not acknowledging my vulnerability, my likeability. (Isn't every human being likeable? Likeable, yes, until he or she flashes a Jim Crow gaze, and the eyes go dead.) If humiliation—as a zone of terrible human possibility—contains mystery and awfulness, its enigma is concentrated in this face I am trying to conjure: the face of the humiliator. Adolf Eichmann's face proposes this enigma. So does Lynndie England's. (One needn't be a mass murderer to be a humiliator.) Michael Jackson's face offers a different puzzle: the child, beaten by his father, became an idol who abhorred his own features and chose, in a ghoulish act of self-erasure and self-creation, to transform them. But I also see, in Michael Jackson's face, the adult man accused of violating children by sleeping with them. And I see the face of a perplexed, unclassifiable man-child humiliated by having his sexual bizarreness or unclassifiability brought into the public eye—Michael Jackson, forced to say "my penis" in an internationally broadcast mea culpa statement, describing how he'd been humiliated by the L.A. police. Everyone knew, everyone could read in the newspaper, that Michael Jackson owned erotica picturing young nude men. This fact become public knowledge.

15.

When President Obama describes, in a speech in Cairo, June 4, 2009, the "daily humiliations—large and small—that come with occupation," he gives the listener cause to lament (with a gloomy sense of lamentation's futility) all the unspeakable occupations that civilizations have undergone in the history of the earth—all the occupations, and therefore all the daily humiliations, large and small. The humiliations undergone by Palestinians, during occupation—different, yes, from the humiliation undergone by a singer like Susan Boyle, or someone less talented than Susan Boyle but deemed to be equally unattractive, a singer appearing on a show like *American Idol* and being laughed at by the callous, snide, Jim Crow–gazed face of the emcee, who laughs along with the audience and prods the spectators into laughter at the fat dowdy woman with bushy eyebrows, a woman who believes she can sing. The humiliation of a derided performer on *American Idol* is immeasurably different from the humiliation of a Palestianian under Israeli occupation. One plight is chosen, the other is not. But isn't there present, in both situations, in the demeanor and behavior of the aggressors, an underlying coldheartedness, a rock-bottom refusal to believe the worthiness of the person whose reputation (or house, or land, or ego, or self-esteem) is stolen, trashed, occupied, razed? Isn't there present, in both situations, an underlying will to deracinate and desubjectify this other person? And, most insidiously—isn't there an insistence on considering this process of desubjectification (*with my laughter I take away your humanity*) an entertaining process, even a cathartic exercise, therapeutic and energizing, like calisthenics? The audience at *American Idol* (or so I hypothesize) experiences laughter as a cosmetic, cleansing procedure—a cheerful exfoliation. I hate group laughter. It is always smug and certain of its position. Lynndie

England's smile and the laughter of the audience at *American Idol* display a callous, morally deadened joviality. Any good soldier must undergo—must grow inured to—this morally deadened state. We spread it elsewhere; we cultivate it at home. Through the enslavement and abuse of African Americans, and the genocide of Native Americans, the United States honed its gift for morally deadened cheerfulness. This self-assured laughter isn't solely U.S. property. It grows elsewhere, too. But it has the quintessentially American tone of mass-media confidence—advertising, commerce, McDonald's, slaughterhouses, or what in the 1960s I learned to call the military-industrial complex. (A stern tone has invaded my sentences: the scourging voice of the educator.)

16.

Is education possible without humiliation? Can we imagine a classroom in which no humiliation, however accidental, ever takes place? (Gentle discipline has virtues: I feel myself rising to the defense of the necessary limits a teacher must impose on a class.) An F is humiliating. So, for perfectionists, is a B+. If the student doesn't feel *doused with corrosive sensation*—if the student doesn't feel *tied to the stake*—then the bad grade isn't humiliating, it's just unfortunate. I felt humiliated, as a student, if the teacher didn't "call on me" when my hand was raised. (*Wayne hogs up too much class time. I'll call on Sam instead.*) Ignored by the teacher, I became instantly the erased, eviscerated body. (*We've heard enough from that loudmouth.*) Fact: I probably humiliate my students every day without knowing it. I wonder if they ever detect, in my face, those telltale traits of amoral indifference that mark the Jim Crow gaze; I wonder if, when my students look at me, they see (even if only for an appalling milli-second) a cold, deadened mask.

THE STINK OF THE LIVERWURST

1.

Today is my little brother's birthday. I often feel that I have inadvertently humiliated him, or I have watched circumstances perform the dirty deed for me. I could be specific about the humiliations he underwent—but by describing them, I would be inflicting further punishment on him. And yet I envied his Gerber baby food jars. I insisted that my mother give me—a seven-year-old—a baby bottle filled with apple juice. I also demanded a pacifier. Its plastic nipple tasted inappropriate. Zest for regression stamped me as already humiliated, even if only in hypothesized eyes.

2.

Jealousy—especially sexual jealousy (why doesn't X love me?)—produces inner reversal. The Siberia/Hades sensation, burning, freezing: *I have been dumped. My beloved—an amplitude, a magnitude—considers me a zero.* (Why so abstract? Why not describe how humiliated I felt when a guy on whom I developed a pointless crush—he was married to a woman, I had no reason to nurse such an extravagant infatuation—dropped me? It's an exaggeration to say I felt humiliated: there were no witnesses. I was the only spectator. But I was seized by the hot/cold sensation, a conviction that his indifference had flash-frozen my body and then blowtorched it.)

3.

Being rejected, and becoming, through one's debased status, a heroine, preoccupies the melodramatic imagination. A scene I can't forget: in Giuseppe Verdi's opera *La Traviata*, the tenor throws his gambling earnings at his ex-girlfriend, a courtesan named Violetta. By hurling cash, he exposes her prostitute nature. Choristers—the assembled crowd—see her pathetically crouching on the floor. The tenor's cruelty humiliates our lady of the camellias—but the outburst humiliates him, too. He sings a few whimpering sotto voce phrases: nearly falsetto, thus emasculated. Postulate: angry outbursts (throwing lucre at a consumptive woman) lead to vocal castration. Witnessing the scene, we relish the heroine's justified self-pity; if she hadn't been humiliated, we would have missed this chance to express our love. Humiliation paves the way for affection: *seeing your abasement, I overflow with love*. Big question: whose side am I on? The spectator's? The humiliated woman's? I hope I don't identify with the creep who hurls money in the courtesan's face.

4.

When King Lear brings onstage his murdered daughter, dead in his arms, not much can be said. He stutters: "Never, never, never, never, never." When Lear dies, not much can be said. A survivor says: "He hates him / That would upon the rack of this tough world / Stretch him

out longer." Imagining the emotions of the characters—
embittered remnants—still onstage after Lear's death,
we gain sudden, bleak insight into *the consolation of aftermath.* Lear is horrified by his daughter's death but
can also relax into the horror, can let it overwhelm and
surround him. And those who watch Lear die can imagine existence as a torture rack on which the old king has
now the good fortune of no longer being stretched. In
this final scene, he realizes, humiliated, that his own
unwise actions caused Cordelia's death. Lear has sunk,
but we might consider him raised—spiritually enriched
by learning the consequences of moral carelessness.
Why am I captivated by ruined men, or men who melo-
dramatically narrate their own ruin?

5.

Shakespeare humiliates the prior body of language—the
poor body of English, lackluster before he came along and
renovated it. Of course, Shakespeare ennobled English,
and so it may seem odd to say that he also humiliated it;
but in his semantic magnanimity, his aural cornucopia,
I detect the presence of lacerations. When Shakespeare
commits lexical excess (by coining new words, by larding
a simple thought with plump, dense sounds and metaphors, by hyper-enlivening every sentiment with figurative language), English becomes a body punctured by his
violent actions. Example: "The murmuring surge / That
on th'unnumb'red idle pebble chafes / Cannot be heard
so high." "Murmuring" and "surge" and "unnumb'red"
present the ear with a glut of "u" and "m" and "r" sounds.
And "idle" and "pebble," next to each other, create a

pebble effect. With purple ripeness, low-pitched vowels
("murmuring surge") ascend to high-pitched vowels
("high"). This apex of virtuosity—language creaming, ascending, and thickening—this process (I'm straining my
point) alerts me to a violence committed, symbolically,
against English's body. Poetic intensity—linguistic bra-
vado, musical compression—hurts the mother tongue.
"Good" language is hurt language. Bare, desiccated
language—Samuel Beckett's—is also humiliated: shorn,
Samson-like. If you don't understand what I'm saying, I
will feel humiliated. If I fail to communicate my meaning,
and if you tell me I've failed, then you will have humiliated me.

6.

In a sonnet, the ratio of humiliation to uplift is 8:6. Eight
lines of humiliation (*I'm a social outcast*); then, the sonnet
undergoes a turn, and the last six lines are uplift, change
of heart (*I'm no longer depressed; I see tomorrow's potential glory*). Shakespeare's sonnet "When in disgrace with
Fortune and men's eyes / I all alone beweep my outcast
state" changes its mind in line nine: "Yet in these thoughts
myself almost depising, / Haply I think on thee, and then
my state / (Like to the lark at break of day arising / . . .)."
Now the speaker remembers his sweetheart and no longer
feels like a dejected loner. Humiliation ends. And so, if we
trust the sonnet form to tell us something about how civilizations have transformed torment into style, and have
organized dejection and consolation into tidy stages and
phases, we will believe that there is an asymmetrical relation between low mood and high mood, between the state

of being outcast and the state of being reabsorbed into relationship; and we will believe that restoration will always follow humiliation, even if humiliation lasts two lines longer than restoration. (Immured in suffering's octave, we yearn for the sestet.) We convert our humiliation into narrative—we exclaim it—in order to experience the stylized, tidal reversal of recuperation, our hearts like the lark at break of day arising.

7.

Anne Sexton felt differently about recuperation. She killed herself by turning on the car's gas and sitting in a closed garage. Her poem "The Death Baby" is a gripping statement of humiliation's seductiveness—its sticky allure. In this poem, she revisits a dream of being locked in a refrigerator. She remembers "the stink of the liverwurst. / How I was put on a platter and laid / between the mayonnaise and the bacon." This smell, this captivity, I can well imagine: I'd feel at home beside liverwurst on an icebox shelf. All of my grand aspirations, my longing for the trance state of a cherub oblivious among clouds in a Veronese or Tiepolo fresco—and look what becomes of me: lodged next to liverwurst. The self always ends up near head cheese, near compressed animal innards; the self must always recognize its likeness to offal, to offal-as-delicacy.

8.

In *Powers of Horror*, Julia Kristeva makes an arresting point about a structure of subordination built into language itself. She says that the "sign"—the word—is an upstairs-downstairs affair, like a fraction whose horizontal line divides a top number and a bottom number. In language's system, the word itself (a set of letters and sounds) rides above the horizontal line; the meaning hides below. (I might be twisting Kristeva's point.) What lies below the line is occluded by the word above, a circumstance of servitude implying that words (as physical objects, as sounds) humiliate their absented meanings. The hard material presence of the word is a husk that humiliates the missing flesh that has been torn from it and left behind as roadkill. I keep circling around linguistic questions, rather than psychological or narrative situations, because whenever I encounter language (and especially when I try to write or read) I'm aware that verbal communication itself involves humiliation. Not merely the humiliation of trying to acquire mastery of a language, or trying to use language accurately and effectively. Not merely the humiliation of not understanding someone else's words, or of feeling like an outcast from the comprehensible and the comprehended. I'm aware, when reading or writing, that the material word's relation to its buried meanings bears humiliation's imprint. The word is victor; its meaning, connotation, implication, and history lie ravished at the conqueror's feet. Or else the word itself seems the victim, the residue, the liverwurst-stink. And the meaning is the unmolested kernel, the aura—the presiding, cerulean intensity.

9.

There is a long tradition of writing about writing's inadequacy—about the necessary failure of words. And certain writers—among them the philosopher Ludwig Wittgenstein, who played games with language but also understood that language's imprecisions and gaps were akin to fleshly amputations—have thought hard, and with a nearly physical sense of agony, about how the act of speaking or writing hurls one to a bottommost realm of incapacity and paralysis. In an apparently innocuous sentence from *Tractatus Logico-Philosophicus,* a neutral sentence that seems to have nothing to do with being humiliated, or suffering injury, or feeling isolated and outcast from the human community, Wittgenstein writes, "The silent adjustments to understand colloquial language are enormously complicated"—and in that simple sentence, the words "silent," "adjustments," "enormously," and "complicated" point to the abyss of lonely incomprehension in which someone alien to a native language must founder. Think of the silent adjustments we all make, the enormously complicated adjustments, merely to have a simple conversation with another human being. Think of the silent adjustments, and the subliminal toll they take on our equanimity, that we must make merely to understand how to behave in front of other people. And think of the humiliation undergone if these silent adjustments are not made. Think of the person who suddenly realizes that he or she may soon be incapable of undergoing the hard work involved in making silent adjustments to standard, consensual idioms of speech and behavior. What if one day I wake up and stop being interested in making these adjustments? To what condition of perpetual humiliation will I henceforth be doomed?

10.

To be assembled in an imaginary library: a canon of humiliated literature, or of literature that embodies—in its aesthetic premises—a state of being humiliated, or of intentionally or unintentionally humiliating the reader. (Also, to be gathered: a canon of humiliated film and visual art.) I prefer literature and art that seems to have been humiliated—where the material texture (paint, imagery, narrative, words, allusions, gestures, color, composition) attests to a *robbed* or *lowered* condition. The writer has experienced debasement; words reverse that state. Or else words enact and continue it. And so the reader feels, *I guess it's not a nightmare to be debased, or else it's a bearable torment, a daily condition.* I don't like confident literature, or literature that seems immune to self-incrimination; literature should bear witness to the fact that the writer was humiliated by the very process of writing the work. The production of language—making words happen—is a lowering act, like revealing my sperm-stained dress at a trial, or showing the judge the inside of my mouth. Language isn't transcendent. Every sentence, however stuffed and upholstered with confident maturity, attests to that earlier, infant time when we couldn't master words.

11.

When Kristeva writes, "language turns into slobber, conversation into defecation," I'm happy. (She is describing Louis-Ferdinand Céline's novel *Journey to the End of the Night,* but the hypothesis applies to language in general, and not merely to the work of this anti-Semitic writer, who embodies, for Kristeva, the glory of abject literature.) I'm glad to see language turn into slobber. Rather, I'm glad to see language forced to admit, "I'm slobber." I'm glad to see language unmastered. And I'm glad to belong to a community, however scattered, of souls who like to see rules (of linguistic propriety, of sexual propriety) turned upside down. When, in Bruce LaBruce's film *Hustler White*, I saw an amputee use his leg stump to penetrate his lover's anus (am I misremembering the scene?), I felt not "grossed out" but filled with a sense of camaraderie—glad to be surrounded, in a Greenwich Village theater, by like-minded perverts. We were a community who felt spacious—roomy, empowered, ample—when greeted by scenes that "normal" viewers would find disgusting. Was the onscreen amputee humiliated or satisfied? How would you describe an audience that finds occasion for laughter, excitement, and *relaxation* when watching amputee anal sex? You might say: we felt, collectively, a warm surge of abreaction, like a hot spring, bubble to the surface of a consciousness fatigued from a lifetime of trying to pretend to comply to the laws of behavioral and aesthetic propriety, a lifetime of making, in Wittgenstein's words, the "silent adjustments," the "enormously complicated" adjustments, necessary "to understand colloquial language" and appropriate sexual behavior. And agreeing to relish the performance of humiliation, either as participant or spectator, may be one paradoxical means of ceasing to comply with these laws. I bring up *Hustler White* to suggest that self-exposure or embarrassment, situations that many people might find painful, are, for others, the occasions for fellow-feeling, for happiness, for release of constraint. I feel the same influx of energy when I watch the antics of Sacha Baron Cohen in *Brüno* or *Borat*—especially the scene when he discovers his co-star, a wiggly, fat, hairy man, masturbating to a photo of Pamela Anderson. "How dare you make hand party over Pamela?" The two men, both nude, end up chasing each other around the hotel. I like to befriend artists and writers who are willing to humiliate themselves, or who understand that slobber and hand party and other outlaw positions may be the result of an aesthetic practice pursued seriously.

12.

In a well-known Robert Capa photo from 1944, a scorned Frenchwoman who'd slept with a German is holding a baby boy in her arms and walking, head punitively shaved, down a village street. Does the baby understand his mother's humiliation, or his own? Village women, confident of their own moral superiority, stare at this scapegoat, this Hester Prynne. Who knows what imprecations they are shouting? No wonder Hetty Sorrel, in George Eliot's *Adam Bede,* kills her baby: better to commit infanticide than to be pilloried as unwed mother, concubine of an occupying Nazi. The Jim Crow gazes of the French villagers, with a confidence I find despicable, define this shorn woman as dirt. Shave her head. Treat her like a Jew. Expel her. I feel her wound, physically, in my stomach, as I look at this photo. And in my chest and nervous system I feel an excited, retaliatory rage at the villagers who are perpetrating this public expulsion. I'm excited to behold polite citizens misbehaving because I know that now they will deserve punishment and I will side with the one-who-punishes; I will wield the whip against the townspeople. Faced with their sin, I experience a combination of grief and exultation. I feel rage, on the woman's behalf, at the villagers; I feel shock that punishment is taking this egregious, visible form; and I feel the bitter thrill of vengeance, as I imagine that these cruel people have now been humiliated forever by Capa's camera. The woman, in the photo, is a Virgin Mary clasping her infant, or a Joan of Arc burning at the stake—an exemplary martyr. I want to kill and punish the villagers who are scapegoating this poor woman. And my retributive, angry wishes suddenly excite me—or I realize that my stimulating rush of horror and anger (provoked by this photo) stems from my own aggression against the villagers, my wish to slaughter them. The Frenchwoman's scapegoating gives me a chance to punish the entire village. No one, in the photo, is looking at Robert Capa. Himself invisible, he has put the expulsed woman, head shaved, with infant, at the composition's center. Suddenly I realize that my mother had short hair when I was a baby and that she married a German. Flashes of reminiscence aren't digressions.

13.

Valley of the Dolls, wig scene, movie version, 1967: in the women's bathroom, Patty Duke pulls off Susan Hayward's wig and tries to flush it down the toilet. "What an awful thing to do to a great star like you," says the bathroom maid, a sympathetic matron, who witnesses

Hayward's disgrace. I discovered Jacqueline Susann's novel when I was in sixth grade. Again and again I read the wig scene, to replay the nightmare: a toilet, home to excrement, is the wrong destination for a wig. In my elementary school's bathroom, the stalls didn't have doors, so I never took a dump there. (Maybe once or twice, in an emergency.) The notion of other boys watching seemed intolerable. The bathroom was dim. One weak bulb? That dungeon was not a place where I could feel at home. Every time I watch *Valley of the Dolls,* I'm horrified when Patty Duke, upstart, dares to pull off Susan Hayward's wig. The terror of the wig going down the toilet: that's why I used to be afraid of bridges. I could imagine losing gravity and flying out of the car window and falling over the Golden Gate Bridge's railing into the San Francisco Bay. Four decades ago, before the Vietnam War escalated, my mother threw my brother's wristwatch out our car window as punishment; and as I write this sentence, I also want to cut it, because I don't want to be caught being too psychological, and I don't want to humiliate my poor mother by fishing into the distant past.

14.

As a kid, I watched a neighborhood girl humiliate my sister with a garden hose. (This recollection may be merely a "screen memory," hence unreliable.) The bully forced my sister to undress, and then sprayed her body with cold water. I watched the scene and didn't protect my sister. However, I sought indirect revenge by squeezing a lemon over the bully's hair. Her last name was Warwick, a word that implied "warlock" and "witch." A

few years later, my sister put gum in her own hair. To
remove the wad, my father (or mother?) cut off the hunk
of hair in which the wad was embedded. This chapter is
full of women who are humiliated by loss of hair. One
more memory: in first grade, a sick schoolmate was half
bald from surgery or chemo. An unfeeling kid made fun
of him, though the teacher had warned us to be kind. I
remember the appalling blank place on the convales-
cent's skull. Recognizability had disappeared into a
void, like a wig flushed down the toilet. He held his head
akimbo; I think he had neurological problems. But the
akimbo posture of the head seemed a sign of his eagerness to belong. When the boy was absent again, for a
long stretch of time, we wrote him get-well notes, and
his sister came to pick up his homework. I felt sorry for
the sister; proximity to the bald kid had tainted her. The
family's name had the syllable "knell" in it, and I was
afraid of that syllable. Nell. Knell. It seemed a shame-
worthy sound. I don't remember ever saying a word to
that sick kid. I only remember being afraid of his last
name, afraid of his sister, afraid of his akimbo head,
afraid of his baldness, afraid of his mysterious absence
from school, afraid of his isolation, afraid of the bulletin
board on which the teacher pinned his response to our
get-well notes. He was one of my first outcasts, but not
the very first. There is no first. The chain of participants
in this collection of outcasts goes back in time to years
before my birth, or your birth, or Julius Caesar's, or
Cain's and Abel's, if we can ever prove that Cain and
Abel really existed. When the Lord had no regard for
Cain, or for Cain's well-meant gift, Cain was furious and

downcast. Genesis says so. "Cain was very wroth, and his countenance fell." We could spend time now brooding over fallen countenances, brooding over what Cain felt, how early it was in human history, and no one there to explain to Cain that God was hard to please and maybe not worth pleasing.

15.

Not downcast, merely nervous, I went on a "date" with a girl, the summer after eighth grade. This was our excursion: we spent the afternoon hanging out at a shopping mall. In a store, some salesperson (the guy who scooped ice cream at Lucky's?) thought I was a girl. "And what flavor would you like, young lady?" It was humiliating to be mistaken for a girl—not because "girl" was a shameful identity, but because it didn't belong to me. I was supposed to be something else, and it—my identity—was supposed to be obvious at first sight. But more compromising was to see my "date," my potential sweetheart, witnessing this mix-up, this disqualification. She rewarded me with a half smile, implying, "This sort of thing often happens to you, Wayne." I'm not sure why I failed at legible boyhood. Long hair? Flowered shirt? Shrimpiness? High voice? Overly enthusiastic body language? Later that afternoon, when our rendezvous ended, I wanted to kiss my "date" good-bye, but instead, afraid, I stood awkwardly beside my bicycle. I contemplated leaning over and kissing her, but she seemed an unbridgeable distance away. I promised to telephone soon. The summer passed, and I didn't keep my promise. Every day, I thought about calling her, just as I thought about ordering (from a magazine ad) a Bullworker isometric muscle builder, to work on my legibility. I wanted to avoid the free fall into genderlessness and hermaphroditism, and I associated this plunge into nothingness with the girl who had witnesssed it, a girl whose first name was a wildflower from the Psalms, and who was born in Germany. She had her own reasons to be humiliated. When I came to her house on the day of our shopping-mall excursion, her father was asleep, though it was nearly noon. She apologized; he had a hangover. That was a new concept for me. A hungover father. Maybe she felt humiliated by her hungover alcoholic German father, as I felt humiliated by the Lucky ice cream scooper mistaking me, in front of a nonplussed witness, for a girl. I apologize for telling you this story.

I WANT TO BE YOUR BITCH

1.

On Craigslist this morning I found: "HAIRY ITALIAN WANTS TO HUMILIATE A GENEROUS BITCH." This hirsute supplicant is "looking to rub my feet all in your face. Sit on your face, spit on you, slap you around." Will he find a "bitch" willing to pay for the pleasure of being mistreated? Another ad: a man wants a man to humiliate him over the phone: "i have a 5 inch skinny dick and i need a big dick man to tell me what a loser and pussy i am, you must be very verbal and very degrading and humiliating." Humiliation, like a pigeon, travels in every conceivable direction: guy ⇒ guy, guy ⇒ girl, girl ⇒ girl, girl ⇒ guy. But because, historically, women have been (let's generalize) more often the recipients of bad treatment—that's the way patriarchy's cookie crumbles—I detect more radical frisson in situations when a man grovels. A bloke asks any chick, on Craigslist, "Humiliate me and my small, bald weenie." Candidly he places his take-out order: "What I need is a woman to make fun of my small, shaved weenie. I need you to tell me how tiny and pathetic it is and how I'll never please any woman with it. I need you to laugh at me as I play with it and try desperately to make it bigger. I need to be told how worthless I am and how no woman would ever be satisfied with my sad excuse for a cock." This chap's a good writer. I'm tickled and impressed by the phrase "my sad excuse for a cock." The search for humiliation, as a leisure sport, is humorous, from a distance, though for its players, up close, the recreation is in deadly earnest.

2.

The Marquis de Sade would have had a field day on Craigslist. His epic chronicle, *The 120 Days of Sodom*, regales the reader with a surfeiting anatomy of humiliations and tortures and ecstasies incomprehensible and beyond the ken of science. Like staring into the sun and going blind, reading Sade's litany of so-called pleasures deadens the imagination by overstimulating it. After reading about the thousandth fuck, the thousandth outrage against the flesh, the hectored traveler can no longer imagine that the human body is an actual apparatus; instead, it seems a fictional battleground, on which any violation can occur, without emotion or consciousness. I give one sample: "He has himself whipped by an old woman, fucks an old man in the mouth, and has the daughter of this aged couple shit into his own mouth, then changes so that, ultimately, everyone takes his turn in each role." Sade's tempo is stately, like a garden-party game of croquet. Each player takes his or her turn; he who humiliates becomes, in a trice, the humiliated party. Death leaves the narrator, and, presumably, Sade's ideal readers, unmoved. Unspeakabilities are poised somewhere between the Spanish Inquisition and Buchenwald, but the Sadean proceeding strikes the tone of Max Ophüls's *La Ronde*—an amoral frolic, without consequence. Beyond the pale of speech, nearly, are Sade's unvisualizable antics. "He cuts off a young boy's four limbs, embuggers the trunk, feeds him well and allows him so to live; as the arms and legs were not severed too close to the body, the boy lives for quite a while. And the surgeon embuggers him steadily for approximately a year." Josef Mengele meets Jeffrey Dahmer: Sade's fictional experiments on the limits of the human may seem remote from the humiliations requested by masochists who post ads on Craigslist, but the continuities are unavoidable, even if Sade's tortured boy, and Sade's heartless surgeon, seem to be mere postulates—figures in a literary farce rather than ingredients in a murderous recipe for the extinction of humankind. I'm not amused by the Marquis de Sade, but I can't deny his clairvoyance, his merciless accuracy about depravity's flora and fauna. A taxonomist of the unendurable, he never reaches his expiration date: the material, though awful, stays fresh.

3.

And why do I spend time reading the Marquis de Sade and the postings of Craigslist humiliation-seekers? Why repeat the words of a guy who says, to the void, to anyone on Craigslist who happens to be listening, "I want to be your bitch"? "I'm looking," this ghostly figure asks, "to be the willing victim of anything a woman has to dish out. Whether you want someone to abuse, or someone to berate and humiliate, or someone to pamper you, or service you, or even just someone to do some chores you've got no interest in doing for yourself, I'm up to it." Armchair psychologist, I'd classify this fellow (how do we know the advertiser is actually male, and not merely

masquerading online as male?) as engaged in an *abreactive* action, a scenario of reparation. He wants to let off
steam, to exorcise a lingering demon. Like the consump-
tion of the host in a Catholic mass, the act of humiliating himself allows this communicant to return to an
earlier, sacred time, a time that might have involved crucifixion and other tortures, but that nonetheless represents what T. S. Eliot serenely called "the still point of the
turning world." The humiliation point—silent, timeless—
never changes; we can only reenter it, registering again at
this strange hotel, signing the guest book, eating the thin
wafer, drinking the familiar glass of wine. The host is always available. Humiliation's gate never shuts, and there
might be (for those who believe in humiliation's creed) a
salvific power in the return to the known, abominable
quarters.

4.

The Buddha's first noble truth was humiliation. (I haven't
yet met the Buddha, though I've sent out an invitation;
one place where I eavesdrop on his teachings is Mark
Epstein's book *Thoughts Without a Thinker: Psychother-
apy from a Buddhist Perspective*.) The human situation—
our captivity to a body—necessarily thrusts us into
humiliation. Epstein writes, "Birth, old age, sickness,
and death are distasteful not just because they are
painful but also because they are humiliating." I don't
think the Marquis de Sade encountered the Buddha; the
marquis had his hands full with Christ. And yet Sade,
devoted to agony's plurality, gives us an inkling that
humiliation is inescapable. Masochists seek it; nonmas-

ochists can't avoid it. Intimacy with humiliation is part of our corporeal inheritance. Emergencies arise, however, when humiliation heaps up and becomes not the counterpoint to pleasure but the totality. I don't want to imagine the sensations of a tortured prisoner—in, for example, Iran, where some prisoners (according to *The New York Times*) said "they had their fingernails ripped off or were forced to lick filthy toilet bowls." In the face of that atrocity, I won't invoke abreaction: nothing salvific about being tortured. Licking filthy toilet bowls is a detail out of Sade; a true Sadean might consider it a mosaic tile in a revolutionary, playful edifice. But on July 29, 2009, this detail is not figment. It is fact.

5.

And from that fact I extract what meaning? You have a right to wonder why I'm drawn to report such details to you—a right to wonder why humiliation is worth contemplating, worth discussing—a right to wonder whether, instead of expatiating on its features, we should simply run away from it, silently.

6.

We assume that the prison guard who demands that the prisoner lick the filthy toilet bowl receives some reward, pleasure, or satisfaction from the demand. We assume that the system of punishment, the state, the structure of power, achieves or believes it achieves results (aggrandizement, entrenchment, consolidation) by such an action. And I presumably achieve results—rhetorical, intangible, egotistical—by repeating the awful story to you.

7.

As an oblique way of addressing the question of why humiliation is worth discussing, I'll tell you another story.
But first, please understand that the only reason I'm
meditating on humiliation is that I recognize its worth,
its indelibility. Humiliation is worthy not because it is
good, or enjoyable, or desirable; humiliation may be ex-
ecrable and unendurable, but it is also genuine. And in a
world that seems increasingly filled with fakeness (is this
an age-old complaint against the incursions of the New?),
humiliation at least rings true.

8.

The story relates not to prisons but to classical music.
When I think about humiliation, I keep returning to classical music; we don't need to revisit Michael Haneke's
The Piano Teacher, with Isabelle Huppert as the sadistic,
erotomaniacal pedagogue, to understand how classical-
music training builds not merely upon delight and aesthetic transport but upon humiliation, whether forestalled
or endured. I return to the subject of classical music because that is where I began my life, my serious life, the life
I still recognize as mine; and it is in the realm of classical
music that I learned how high the stakes could be when a
person wanted to try to make something beautiful, and
how perilous the fall and the humiliation could be when
the attempt failed.

9.

A fellow piano student, at a summer music school, told
me this story. One of the school's teachers, a beloved

instructor, whose specialty was "relaxation" (I approached her, once, to ask for special advice on how to relax my shoulders when I played, because my shoulder tension was a terrible problem, oft-mentioned by onlookers, sometimes charitably, sometimes mockingly)—this teacher, whose specialty was "relaxation" (I'm not sure how I figured out this fact, except through the school's rumor mill), made her debut playing the Schumann Piano Concerto with an orchestra in London. Or at least she tried to make her debut. She arrived onstage, bowed to the clapping audience, sat down at the piano. And then (or so the horrified student told me) she threw up on the keyboard. That was the end of the performance. And that was the end of her career as concert pianist.

10.

That story might be apocryphal. Maybe she didn't throw up. Maybe she wiped up the vomit with a handkerchief and continued with the performance. But, like the Buddha's first noble truth, the story, in its received form, told me something important about performance, about classical music, about failure and success, about ambition, and about bodies. Bodies vomit—even in concert halls, far from the cloistered sickroom. Classical music demands repeatable, foolproof perfection. Expressivity, playfulness, spontaneity—these virtues, too, have a place in classical music performance. But perfection—or a level of professional competence so high that very few can achieve it—is required. Standards of that intensity and rigor leave most of us by the wayside. Nerves sabotage the cult of perfection. The body humiliates us, or threatens to, just at those moments when we wish to come across as bodiless, immune to failure. The pianist wanted to play the Schumann Piano Concerto as if she were not a person with a stomach and a digestive tract. But her gut, and her nervous system, spoke more loudly than her ambition. Her nausea—and her unconscious—asserted itself as more important than her aesthetic aims, her love of Schumann, or her technical prowess. A piano keyboard is a sobering object. The keys, especially if made of ivory, are clean and shiny. Vomit, however, is ugly and smelly. Vomit is the epitome of an abject substance—a material that should remain unseen and inward, but that ejects itself, is thrust outward, into the public, visible realm. Vomit on the keyboard—that image symbolizes, for me, the always possible danger of the body speaking up for its own rights, against the stringent demands of the mind's wish to construct a plausible, attractive, laudable self for other people to consume.

11.

Performance's First Noble Truth: you may wish to play the Schumann Piano Concerto, but you might vomit instead. And therefore do not count on the performance to go well. Do not expect to be admired. At bottom you are capable of ejecting—thrusting outward—vile matter that the audience will interpret as equal to your body. You are the vomit you've spewed onto the keyboard. And that vomit will never leave you; it will mark you for the rest of recorded time.

12.

Once, ill-advisedly, when I was sixteen, my trumpet teacher got me a gig, despite my mediocre attainments: he arranged for me to be the soloist in "Fantasy and Variations on 'The Carnival of Venice'" with a local band at a public park. In preparation for the first rehearsal with the band, I met the conductor—an Italian man whose name sounded like Arturo Toscanini—for a coaching session. The maestro, after hearing me play, diagnosed my problem: "You have no knowledge of bel canto. You're not playing melodically." My breathing was spastic. Soon after this disastrous session, the bandleader fired me. My teacher broke the news: "You wouldn't want to be the worst soloist of the summer, would you?" I didn't tell my parents that I'd been bumped. I lied: "The concert got canceled." *The worst soloist of the summer*: I escaped that humiliation. But I earned, instead, the humiliation of knowing that I *would have been* the worst. That's a polite way of saying "I was the worst." I'm not trying to pose as the world's most wounded ex-trumpeter; I'm simply bearing witness to an insult's unstoppable reverberations. I'll wager that most human beings on earth—those of us who are not enlightened and may never become enlightened—hear such phrases, such humiliating refrains, every day, as the background music to our lives.

13.

A succinct request appears on Craigslist. The subject heading is "HUMILIATE ME." The ad itself: "I want to be humiliated today. Tell me what you want to do to me. In detail. Thanks." The guy sounds polite. His application for abuse is genial. Another man, a twenty-six-year-old Italian, wants to be humiliated to the extreme. He offers the applicant specific suggestions: "tease and torment me without relief"; "piss all over me"; "make another guy fuck you and make me eat his cum out or drip it on me"; "have your friends come by and tease and make fun of me." He weighs 245 pounds. He says, "I am looking for utter humiliation and loss of all control." I'm still uncertain why I consider it necessary—and cathartic—to report to you that there are men who seek humiliation as a form of reparation, of sexual stimulation, and of psychological bookkeeping. Humiliation, within the masochistic economy, cancels a prior debt. The pursuit of humiliation—as sport, as mental hygiene—is a slow, regular practice; we do it again and again, our technique improving with every rehearsal, every audition. Freud would have called this behavior a repetition compulsion; he acknowledged that the compulsion to repeat the same thing, even a painful thing, satisfies an instinct greater than the will to pleasure. And although the advertiser on Craigslist who begs to be teased and tormented may seem to be obeying his own will, Freud argued that none of us are entirely in control of our performances. There may be nothing volitional about our return—whether in the name of abreaction, salvation, anesthesia, or "kicks"—to humiliation's infernal region.

14.

The poet Eileen Myles, in an essay boldly titled "Everyday Barf," remembers saying "vomit" in class—as provocation—and being punished by the teacher. Myles recalls "the raucous sound of the classroom laughter. Even I joined in, feeling entirely out of control, humiliated, but the enormous release the one word had triggered still made me snort and gag with pleasure." I doubt that the pianist whose botched debut consisted of vomiting on the keyboard enjoyed the same release that Myles achieved by saying "vomit"; but drawing near to an awful experience, without actually undergoing it, can feel cathartic. Playing with matches isn't the same as enjoying a burn. Thus, we may perversely entertain ourselves by watching spectacles of other people's humiliation, or by dwelling on our own past disasters; or we may experiment by committing a new disgrace. I may blurt out the word "vomit," even though the class guffaws in scorn—or maybe in envy. Some of us admire outcasts and outlaws; humiliation qualifies an applicant for membership in either tribe. But we don't choose to become outcasts, even if we repeat the behavior that led to our expulsion, and even if, with each repetition, we embroider the scene with showy cadenzas.

15.

Two years in a row—third grade, fourth grade—I threw up in school. Both inadvertencies occurred midautumn, in the morning. Each time, seized by dizziness and malaise, I'd walk (nearly passing out) to the teacher's desk; unable to speak, I'd vomit into her wastebasket. I remember the look of the basket's interior, as I leaned over; some puke landed on her desk and on the floor. I don't remember other students laughing. But I remember thinking that someone—teacher, janitor?—would be forced to mop up my mess. After each accident, a classmate led me to the principal's office, where a secretary telephoned my mother to come pick me up. Those episodes—far in the past, and not catastrophic—marked me, however momentarily, as a vomiter, as a boy who couldn't keep his sickness away from the public eye and who ruined the classroom with his filth. Therefore—in the world as I see it, to this day— the possibility of vomiting in public remains (symbolically) an awful imminence, which casts, over civilized life, a shadow. I'm worried not only about my own collapse; I'm worried about everybody's. I'm worried about *all of us* losing control; our civilized veneer—the illusion that we are decent and clean—might, at any moment, crack. And such a breakdown, for any of us, would be humiliating—for the person collapsing, and for those of us forced to watch the expulsion, the dreck. If Kafka were to rise from the dead and ask me to describe my personality in the most general terms, I would oblige the master by telling him that I am a person who exercises care with respect to his fluids and solids, his ingestions and expulsions. I place a high premium on not ever again letting myself explode in public, on not ever again letting myself be lowered in public to the level of a body out of control, expelling foul matter. I'd rather crawl into a hole and vanish, like a nearly voiceless specter from the world of Samuel Beckett: "Throw up and go. Where neither. Till sick of there. Throw up and back. The body again. Where none. The place again. Where none. Try again. Fail again." Here, in his novella *Worstward Ho,* and elsewhere in his work, too, Beckett's credo is basic black: "Try again. Fail again. Fail better." A grim victory, that one word, "better," and I don't know if I believe its spartan consolation. There is no better. We try again and again to escape humiliation. And then we are thrust, with a shudder, back into our bodies, a place where the script never changes: the script says fail, says die, says foul. No escaping the wastebasket.

THE BLOB

1.

Susan Sontag wrote eloquently about the moral complexities of looking at photographs of other people's suffering. And then she died. Annie Leibovitz took photos of her dying, and photos of her corpse, and published them. They are difficult to look at. I've never seen a dead body, except at a wake, after the body has been primped and prettied. My friend John, an aesthete, died of AIDS; I saw his corpse. Two other corpses I've seen: the mother of my friend Glenn, a painter; and the brother of my friend Lazarus, an architect. At Anna Moffo's wake, which I attended, the casket was closed. The photos of dead Sontag confused and frightened me. At first I didn't understand that the recumbent object was a dead body; I thought it was an expensive effigy, an Egyptian antiquity, a statue carved out of a tree trunk. Then I realized that this dark lump was Sontag. Here's how her son, David Rieff, in his book *Swimming in a Sea of Death*, described the effect of those photos: his mother was "humiliated posthumously by being 'memorialized' that way in those carnival images of celebrity death taken by Annie Leibovitz." Rieff's use of the word "humiliated" deserves pondering. Can one be humiliated posthumously? If Sontag isn't alive to experience the indignity, is she actually being humiliated? The disfigurements of

illness, the bloating and discoloration of death: I understand Rieff's point, I reckon how humiliating it would be
to know that someone is seeing my body when it has
grown ugly and unrecognizable and not quite human,
when it has become a piece of sacred rubbish. Trying to
figure out whether dying and death are humiliating, and
for whom they are humiliating (the survivors? the witnesses?), I begin to examine my attitudes toward disfigured or impaired bodies, which have, at times, inspired
in me a combination of voyeuristic curiosity and physical horror. Recently at the grocery store I saw a woman
whose mottled face was swollen to twice the size of a
"normal" face. I don't know the name for her condition,
but I know that she wore fashionable shoes and well-
fitting jeans that showed off her svelte waistline and
shapely buttocks. I also noticed the fine material of her
sweater—cashmere?—and I wondered how she coped
with the stares of other people; I wondered whether I
would be doing her more of an injustice by looking away
from her face or by neutrally noticing it, perhaps even
smiling or establishing friendly eye contact. I felt, wrongly
or rightly, that my presence, in the grocery store, as a non-
disfigured person, who might have self-conscious and self-
lacerating attitudes toward his own appearance but who
had no medically acknowledged abnormalities of feature,
intensified this woman's humiliation. And I remembered a freakish kid in my neighborhood when I was
growing up: my brother and I referred to him as the Blob
because he had a lumpy jaw—as if a golf ball had lodged
between his lower lip and his chin. I sometimes saw the
Blob at Safeway supermarket with his mother; I was

afraid to look directly at him, afraid that I would some-
how get infected by his deformity if I acknowledged
him. Whether he was "retarded" or merely "deformed" I
couldn't ascertain, but I knew that I belonged to the social engine that had inadvertently or deliberately humiliated him, even if he'd never heard me say, "Look! There's
the Blob!," even if he'd never seen my hilarious Blob
impersonation—tongue crammed beneath a distended
bottom lip, jaw protruding like a dog's muzzle.

2.

Earlier, I asserted that humiliation is always a triangle:
tyrant, victim, witness. In the case of the Sontag photos,
the photographer (Leibovitz) is the unwitting tyrant, Sontag is the victim, and we (the viewers) are the witnesses. But the humiliation happens not inside Sontag's
body, which no longer exists, but inside our bodies,
watching. Indeed, the humiliation doesn't actually happen; it is a cloud of inference and aftermath, a nonlocat-
able atmosphere of outrage and distress. We use the word
"humiliation" sometimes merely rhetorically, to describe
a potential for agony, even if the agony is not always, in
that instant, an actual experience; in these cases, humiliation can't be touched, measured, visualized, or weighed.
When I saw the disfigured woman at the grocery store,
humiliation didn't actually exist. It hadn't yet taken form
as a scene of violence or insult or rejection; rather, humiliation was merely an imminence—the danger that
someone might treat this woman in a hurtful way. Vulnerability cast a cloud over her—call it a storm cloud, a
constant threat of rain, and the rain that threatened to

fall was humiliation. It never fell, as I far as I could tell, but I was powerless to prevent it from falling. I did not humiliate the woman at the grocery store, though witnessing her vulnerability showered me with discomfort, as if I, the witness, were "catching" humiliation from her—or else wrongfully imputing it to her, burdening a stranger with my own fears.

3.

And now, without apology, but with considerable dread, I turn to lynching photographs—souvenir images taken of the flayed, burned, gouged, dismembered corpses of black men, and sometimes women, in the South. That such grisly photographs exist proves that white people were happy to stand near the disfigured corpses; white perpetrators and bystanders were proud to murder and then to gloat. (I stop writing, and look again at the photographs. I keep looking. The longer I look, the more I lose my grip on words.) These photographs show that white people believed the event—torture and murder—worth commemorating and communicating. The word "humiliation" seems inadequate to describe the atrocity of lynching; and yet, before the torture and mutilation ended (and sometimes it lasted for hours), before the sanctioned exercise of mass sadism came to a conclusion, if the effects of such cruelties ever end, the desire to humiliate must have been among the motives of the murderers. The lynching photographs—limit-case images, which call into question what it means to look at a photograph and what it means to be an American—document and perpetuate the white reign of terror; they continue the work of bringing blacks down, of advertising and entrenching their subordination, of "desubjectifying" blacks, perpetuating their humiliation, and foreclosing liberation. The photos don't merely record acts of humiliation and violence; they perform and extend the damage. They make horror happen again. The photos are of dying and dead bodies, but the photos are alive. They can't be put to sleep. Hilton Als, in his essay "GWTW," included in *Without Sanctuary: Lynching Photography in America,* speaks candidly about the continuities he senses between lynching photographs and his own experiences of being looked at by white people. Als: "Of course, one big difference between the people documented in these pictures and me is that I am not dead, have not been lynched or scalded or burned or whipped or stoned. But I have been looked at, watched, and it's the experience of being watched, and seeing the harm in people's eyes—that is the prelude to becoming a dead nigger like those seen here, that has made me understand, finally, what the word 'nigger' means, and why people have used it, and the way I use it here, now: as a metaphorical lynching before the real one." Cruelly watched, he has seen "the harm in people's eyes." In that eye-to-eye moment of confrontation, he has received the warning. I've called it the Jim Crow gaze—the moment of being seen as naught, of realizing that you aren't being viewed as a person but as rotting meat, as excrescence, as future corpse. When the Jim Crow gaze lands on your devalued body, you have been brought unspeakably, irreversibly low—thrust downward to a point so below the human that you will never again find a chance to rise. After

Cambridge police arrested Harvard professor Henry Louis Gates, Jr., caught entering his own house (a neighbor, imagining that Gates was a burglar, had called the police), Bob Herbert wrote, in an editorial in *The New York Times,* that "black people are constantly being stopped, searched, harassed, publicly humiliated, assaulted, arrested and sometimes killed by police officers in this country for no good reason." Humiliation of black people in the United States is a system; the system includes prisons, police, hospitals, schools, the food chain. The system, an ecology, includes you, whoever you are, and it includes me. I regret that in my eyes it may be possible for a black person to imagine harm and to see nonrecognition, dismissal, fear, dismay, longing, identification, curiosity. I have been guilty of looking at a black person in such a way that my face and my body have registered, however unintentionally and unconsciously, the moral morass of being *the white person watching the black person*; and because my body and my face can't do much to take away the implicit stain of being a *white person looking at a black person,* my gaze becomes the Jim Crow gaze, or an inheritor of the history of that gaze, and my eyes, however kind or inquisitive or disinterested or unaware of their effect, give the wheel of humiliation another fateful turn. Some necessary shame and guilt reside in my gait and gaze, the demeanor of someone who knows he contributes to the problem, who knows he is involved in humiliating others, simply because it is my white face that is doing the watching; and a face, like mine, that anyone could tell from a mile away was Ashkenazi Jewish, doesn't forfeit whiteness, at least not at this moment in the history of prejudice.

4.

From my four years at a public high school in a California suburb, I recall the presence of only one black student. Perhaps there were others—but I remember only one, a quiet girl who wore what I remember as a nice sweater and whose skin was not very dark but only slightly dark. After a year or two, she disappeared. I assume that she transferred to another school, or else that her family moved. I am more surprised at the absence of any emotion or concern from this memory of my high school's demographics than I am by the memory itself.

5.

In first or second grade, unprompted, I wrote a tiny book. I got the idea by reading a biography of Harriet Tubman; the scene when the overseer hits Tubman with an anvil—leaving a dent on her forehead—made a dent on my imagination. I could imagine the weight of that anvil, and the indelibility of its mark on her skull. I could almost imagine the sensation of that heavy anvil falling upon me. And so I wrote a story, drew some pictures, made a cover, stapled the pages together, and deemed it a book. I wanted to call it *Slavery Is Awful,* but I misspelled the adjective. My accidental title became *Slavery Is Aval.* Maybe I was trying to bring "awful" closer to "anvil." I have always been curious about humiliation; certain representative instances of suffering and damage—the anvil hurled at the slave's forehead— struck me as extreme parables for ordinary humiliations. To take Harriet Tubman as allegory of quotidian punctures to self-esteem is not a morally decent thing to do; but it is exactly what I did. And when, in sixth grade, our teacher, a white woman who'd taught in Harlem (so she told us), recited a Langston Hughes poem ("I, Too, Sing America"), I took the poet's plight personally. When he said, "I am the darker brother," I took notice. I thought, *I have two brothers, and my skin is slightly darker than theirs. So maybe I'm the "darker brother."* The darker brother, Hughes wrote, eats "in the kitchen / When company comes." My whole family ate every meal in the kitchen, at the white Formica kitchen counter, and so I wondered why Hughes considered it exceptional or odd that he must eat in the kitchen when company came. I hadn't yet learned about dining rooms. Nor had I learned about metaphor.

6.

We take other people's ordeals seriously as an emblem for our own, lesser humiliations. A believer notices Christ's crucifixion and takes interpretive, imaginative liberties with it. A believer says, "I'm not being crucified, but this fever—this divorce—this foreclosure—this lawsuit—this insult—feels like Calvary." Maybe just knowing that you will eventually die feels like crucifixion. Maybe knowing that you will become a bloated, disfigured corpse, and that someone who doesn't care about you (hospital attendant, mortician, heir) will move your dead body into the proper position for a dead body to occupy— maybe this knowledge, that a stranger or a lover will one day find your body disgusting and smelly, and will want to dispose of it quickly, is a way of taking Christ's lynching personally. The turn toward religion—and toward the salvific interpretation of suffering (imagining that humiliation can be alchemized, redeemed)—reveals a perfectly human wish to seek correspondences between lower and higher, left and right, blighted and whole; whether religious or not, we aren't wrong to ask that small events find their meaning through comparison with larger events.

7.

I read Richard Wright's *Black Boy,* in seventh grade, because my mother suggested it. She was trying to rescue me from a bad choice I'd made. I'd already chosen another book, and read it, and written my report. The book I'd chosen was *See No Evil,* based on a movie starring Mia Farrow, who plays a blind woman. (Shades of Audrey Hepburn in *Wait Until Dark*? I found glamorous thin blind women in movies to be handy emblems of what a terrified soul endures when moored—for a life's sentence—inside an unyielding body.) My mother said, "*See No Evil* isn't a book. It's a novelization. Read *Black Boy* instead." Feeling ashamed that I'd had the poor taste to think *See No Evil* a proper subject for a book report, I buckled down to reading *Black Boy* in our tract house's backyard; lying on the lawn, I immersed myself in the young narrator's sufferings and shames. Identification hit immediately: when he accidentally sets fire to his house—the first scene in the book—and recognizes, "I had done something wrong, something which I could not hide or deny," merely because he'd "wanted to see how the curtains would look when they burned," I took Richard Wright's accidental act of arson, and his ensuing sense of original sin ("I had done something wrong"), as emblems for a humiliation I believed was intrinsic to the state of being a child. And when Wright learns that the larger humiliations he will encounter are not at the hands of his mother but at the hands of the white world—when he learns "how to watch white people, to observe their every move, every fleeting expression, how to interpret what was said and what left unsaid," I understood his wariness, and felt (no doubt wrongly) that *Black Boy* could be my guide to underdog consciousness, or what it felt like to look at the world with the assumption that the world disapproved of your existence. When, because his white coworkers persecute him, Richard Wright's narrator quits his job at the optical company, he feels humiliated by the gaze of the "white stenographer" watching him. Richard is afraid to tell his boss about the racial assaults of his white coworkers, and so he says nothing to vindicate himself: "The white stenographer looked at me with wide eyes and I felt drenched in shame, naked to my soul. The whole of my being felt violated, and I knew that my own fear had helped to violate it." This is the sensation I've tried to describe earlier as the "inner fold," the sensation of horrid internal reversal or self-revulsion; as a result of this scene of humiliation, Wright notices, "for weeks after that I could not believe in my feelings. My personality was numb, reduced to a lumpish, loose, dissolved state. I was a non-man, something that knew vaguely that it was human but felt that it was not." Maybe now we'd call his condition post-traumatic shock. But he's not yet post-traumatic. The trauma will continue for decades.

I haven't finished grappling with my possibly immoral use of Richard Wright and Harriet Tubman, in my youth, as extreme magnifications of the petty humiliations I felt; nor have I precisely landed on the "I am a corpse" feeling (or "I am seen as a corpse"), a deathly foretaste that seems woven into the experience of humiliation. When I first read *Black Boy,* I did not consider myself a member of a sexual minority; however, I considered myself the inhabitant of a body that was strange to itself, uncomfortable with its form and appearance, and at once hypersensitive to nuances of sensation (palpation, temperature, texture, taste) and deadened to so much else within and without that body that I don't know how to begin even to give a name to this experience of deathliness-within-life. Or was I aware, as a child, that others around me were also dead to themselves, and thus dead—at least in discontinuous flickers of time—to others, to me?

8.

I've watched several times, on YouTube, a video clip of four male homosexuals throwing a pie in the face of homophobe Anita Bryant at a televised news conference, 1977, Des Moines. Before the pie throwing occurs, she confidently describes her crusade to do away with gay people. After a bearded activist thrusts—audibly, violently—a pie into Bryant's face, she says, "At least it's a fruit pie," and bows her head and entreats God: "Father . . . we're praying for him to be delivered from his deviant lifestyle." But then she starts crying, as gobbets of fruit pie trickle down her face. I'm no fan of Anita

Bryant, who did harm to queers. But I cringe, watching the fruit pie slam into her unsuspecting face. Suddenly, she is no longer a wretched antigay activist. Suddenly, she is a victim, a woman physically assaulted by a male stranger. White cream, the pie's topping, covers her features; it resembles shaving foam or whiteface makeup. A few seconds ago, she was a wrong-minded, wrong-acting bigot, but now she has become a humiliated woman, crying in public. I can imagine how wretched I'd feel if someone threw a pie at me; in the capillaries of my cream-coated, humiliated face, I'd sense the aggression and hatred that motivated the pie-hurling hand. That's why I don't believe in capital punishment: any murderer weeping and shivering with humiliated fear at the oncoming electrocution earns my clemency. Anita Bryant put her orange-juice fame ("Come to the Florida Sunshine Tree") to noxious uses, but when the pie hits her face and she weeps, she becomes a horrifying, human spectacle, a white body smeared with white crap. During the awful instant when Anita Bryant breaks down crying, I suddenly feel guilty for my own aggression against her. Even when I want to see someone punished, I feel remorse when the disciplining occurs. I remember how sickening it felt to hear my brother and sister crying. I remember how like an "inner fold" (a twisted seam of revulsion) it felt to hear my brother and sister weeping because they had been punished, whatever "punishment" meant, and it was never corporal; I remember hearing my mother cry because she felt her life was no longer her own. For her disenfranchisement I felt responsible. I may have momentarily hated her and wanted her to die, but when she cried, even if her sadness was mixed with rage, I believed that my misbehavior had ruined her, and I felt humiliated by that knowledge, dragged into the mucus and muck of her tears, tears that I'd provoked, witnessed, relished, and rued.

FIVE O'CLOCK SHADOW

1.

I feel physically disgusted after watching several episodes in a row of the now-canceled reality TV show *The Swan*. I often don't like my appearance (recently, in a failed poem, I confessed, "My nose, chin, neck, cheeks, hair: none are up to par"), but I generally don't consider these deficits humiliating. The women who opt to appear on *The Swan*, however, who sign up for plastic surgery and undergo the procedure and the recovery on camera, who elect to receive tummy tucks and cheek implants and brow lifts so that they might compete in a beauty pageant against the other renovated "ugly ducklings"—these women feel humiliated by their bodies. "I think I look ugly," says one. And a plastic surgeon proclaims: "Marnie has a tired look . . . she does not have much shape to her calves." Medical ethics fly out the window. "Dawn really needs more feminization. And that's the goal with the surgery. If we can achieve that, she can be a really pretty girl." I need more masculinization, but no one ever suggested I get plastic surgery. While I was growing up, my main gripes against God were that I was Jewish and short; neither characteristic could be repaired by surgery. However, I straightened my kinky hair—a source of shame—by wearing a beanie cap at night and by spreading ChapStick on wayward tresses during the day. Self-hating Dawn agrees with the surgeon's assessment: "Anything's better than this," she opines about her current, pre-op appearance. How upbeat and utopian these televised surgeons are, confident that Dawn's humiliations can be erased and reversed with a scalpeling and a suctioning: "The fact that one breast was so much smaller and droopier than the other breast had to be a source of major anxiety for Dawn. Today we're going to end all that." These disturbed women ask to be humiliated on television so that they might end up beautiful—but after surgery's purgatory they end up resembling Jocelyn Wildenstein, a tabloid curiosity, a compromise between lynx and socialite. The deeper the delusion, the more entertaining the show. The woman's self-disgust is a prized commodity; we're supposed to be amused by her disconnection from reality, amused—or riveted with horrified fascination—by her self-destructive search for chimerical, surgically achieved equilibrium. Isn't the most wretched aspect of *The Swan* the women's self-disparagement in the presurgical sequences, when the candidates for transformation weep about their droopy asses and the gaps between their teeth, when they confess that a desire for invisibility compels them to drive cars with tinted windows, and when, on camera, they shave unwanted facial hair? Isn't the most stigmatizing spectacle their willingness to appear in public saying, "I'm ugly"? A pathetic subject breaks down weeping as she describes being humiliated by high-school bullies, who pushed the girl into her locker. "My facial hair became a problem," says a sad sack. One sacrificial lamb is commanded to undergo a brow lift, an upper lip lift, liposuction under the eyes, liposuction under the chin, fat transfer to cheeks,

Lasik eye surgery, breast augmentation, tummy tuck, bleaching of teeth, veneers, gum surgery, root canals, deep cleaning, a 1,700-calorie-a-day diet, two hours a day at the gym, and weekly therapy. Her crime? She considers herself ugly. And the surgeon collaborates in her delusion: he thinks that "breast augmentation" and a "tummy tuck" will "really bring out her playfulness." At what price playfulness?

2.

And so why do I feel sick watching this show? (Some viewers, I admit, might not feel sick; some might consider it merely entertaining. But I have never been an advocate of funny games.) TV in general makes me queasy: I'm revolted by how transparently the contestants and emcees, on game shows and other "reality" fare, seem consoled and cocooned by the attention the camera (and the studio audience) gives them. The specimens on *The Swan,* in particular, seem eager to confess, on camera, their misery. One woman wears a hyperunflattering pair of overalls; she compliantly occupies the dire first half of the punitive Before/After diptych. Doesn't she know that by simply wearing a better outfit, she could leap into the triumphant After, without the mortification of surgery? To understand why viewers are excited or moved by seeing the parade of humiliation, we'd need to look beyond psychology; we'd need to examine the flow of capital, which encourages "false consciousness" in consumers, duped into believing that a woman who becomes more "feminine" (which, on *The Swan,* means losing weight, truncating the nose, fixing the breasts, and becoming blond) will alter her destiny and achieve happiness. If, for a moment, her dream is fulfilled (for three months she lives in isolation, in rooms without mirrors, so she can't see herself, until, in the final, broadcast ceremony, a mirror is unveiled and she beholds the results of surgery and makeover)—if, for a moment, the woman seems thrilled, and weeps with joy to witness her transformed features, this visible pleasure humiliates her, because we know it is founded on myth. More accurate, and honest, is the moment when an aspiring swan appears on camera, in the hospital, after plastic surgery, her face bruised and unrecognizable: she croaks, in a voice thickened by anesthesia and trauma, "Please keep medicine in me. I don't want to wake up."

3.

A conceptual humiliation we all suffer is complicity with a culture—a media nation—that propagates shows like *The Swan.* I'm more disgusted by the blather of the experts than by the footage of dental surgery. Even a mouth gaping open and bleeding, in a periodontal close-up, isn't as repellent as the program's coach, yelling at a disobedient contestant who reneged on her diet by gorging on cream cheese and a pack of hot dogs: "If you don't change your eating habits, you're going to be a tub when you get home!" The sordid feeling that arises when I watch *The Swan* reminds me of the sympathetic revulsion I experienced, long ago, watching a little girl throw up in a car traveling along curvy mountain roads. Smelling my friend's puke, I started gagging. I was disgusted by her loss of bodily control, but this disgust produced in me a reflex imitation, a mimic loss of agency. And so I propose a theorem: watching another person's humiliation, we reproduce that horror in our own bodies. Our mirror neurons fire. We become the beheld horror. We cede ownership and custody of our corporeality when we witness someone else's surrender. When I try to imagine the sensations of bystanders to a lynching, an execution, a public flaying, I presume that these watchers experienced a vicarious, physical horror that they transmuted into excitement, anger, and indignation. Here, I can offer only intuition, and the evidence of my senses, which indicate that the disgust felt by the witness of humiliation (or by me, when I witness a televised pillory, or a girl vomiting in a car's backseat) is a peculiar combination of rage and helplessness: my rage at the material implacability of bodies, which produce automatic responses like vomiting or tears; and my helplessness as spectator of a suffering I did not cause, and as a mortal whose own body must eventually surrender to decay. To be seen surrendering: that is humiliation. And to witness someone else's surrender: that might be triumph, but it might also sicken the beholder.

4.

My primal scene of spying on someone else's surrender was watching Richard M. Nixon resign the presidency on TV. I remember my glee and shock at seeing the physically and morally unappealing head of the country give up his power. Maybe I took the resignation personally because of Nixon's five o'clock shadow, which reminded me of my father's face. Nixon resigning—the commander in chief humiliated—seemed a quintessential father-brought-low moment. I might have pitied Nixon, or pitied the man with the five o'clock shadow, but I also relished his punishment, his shame. This complicated surge—feeling horrified that the powerful man should lose his eminence, but also feeling gleeful that he must display his downfall—lives in me still as a queasy avidity, connected with a man's beard, or the seeming incongruity of a shave-worthy man exposed to public shunning. *Shun the man who shaves; humiliate the hirsute.* That was my clarion call—rousing me to excitement but also to remorse and grief.

5.

Richard Nixon, resigning, mentions his body, and mentions the horror that fills a body when it stands on the threshold of humiliation and knows it must dive into the vortex. Nixon says, "I have never been a quitter. To leave office before my term is completed is abhorrent to every instinct in my body." Odd, that the president should mention his body: Watergate wasn't a sexual scandal, but it manifested as physical abhorrence. "Therefore I shall resign the Presidency effective at noon tomorrow": the defeated man dictates his own execution. Noon—high noon—becomes a punishment word, a slated, destined termination. Watching this speech again, more than thirty years later, I still imagine that I am his daughter Tricia, listening with pride and horror.

6.

That horror will always continue. There will always be another public figure falling, another man, closely shaved or needing a shave, a man in a good suit, a broad-shouldered man with a receding hairline and jowls, or a slump-shouldered man with a narrow chin and an unusual nose, to confess, in public, a shameful act, and to submit to the televised spanking, the head bowed, the wife, always the wife, and maybe the daughter, too, standing beside him. "I am deeply sorry that I did not live up to what was expected of me," says New York governer Eliot Spitzer, who was discovered to have paid an exorbitant sum for sex with a prostitute whom he transported across state lines. Beside penitent Eliot stands his wife, Silda, whose scarf is correct and silk and noncompensatory: its impeccability can't ameliorate her shame and therefore seems to intensify it. Here's what one anonymous Internet commentator says, responding to the YouTube clip of the shame speech: "I can't believe this horndog loser dragged his wife up on stage to be humiliated even more than she already is. Silda, wake up and dump this loser." Eliot admits, on camera, "The remorse I feel will always be with me," and while he apologizes, I become preoccupied by one analogy: his head looks like a penis, and his penis is what got him in trouble. Silda's gaze has two options: it may wander, or it may stay fixed on the horizon. I watch her eyes for signs of life, anger, opinion, and receive no clues, or only the evidence of toleration and endurance: the fact that she meets the requirement to remain proper and exact and mannerly in public, and to refrain from keening and excoriation, attests to her dignity but also amplifies her humiliation. Eliot, trying to put a positive spin on his humiliation, perorates: "Our greatest glory consists

not in never falling, but in rising every time we fall."
Spitzer's resignation aria is a bar mitzvah speech seen
through a glass darkly: the boy ascending into puberty
and membership in the community has now become
the man-boy descending into ignominy, into "private
life," into the head-bowed-low posture of the scolded
and the slapped.

7.

I refused to have a bar mitzvah because I considered my
older brother's bar mitzvah a humiliating experience.
(From a bad case of internalized anti-Semitism I'm slowly
recovering.) The melismatic, chanting voice, moving in
irregular, unpopular directions, seemed obscene; its beauty
and dignity were lost on me. I considered it humiliating to
be a Jew. None of my friends were Jews. In second grade,
my teacher said, on the first day of Chanukah, "Wayne is a
Jew. He can explain Chanukah to us." I couldn't explain it.
I didn't even try.

8.

Though guilty of turning against my own people, I am
disgusted by Jew-hating comments on the Internet about
the Spitzers (one post calls the ex-governor a "hideous
money hungry jew," another says "jewish Silda wanted
furs, jewelry, and money"): the tone of talk radio, too, is
pitched at this ignorant, angry level of rant and accusa-
tion, and I want no part of it. Aggressive public speech
humiliates the mouth that utters it, or the hands that type
and transcribe and publish it.

9.

"I did nothing wrong at the Minneapolis airport," says Senator Larry Craig, busted for "lewd conduct" in a men's room stall—he bumped his foot in a sexually suggestive semaphore (code for "let's have sex") and reached his hand under the partition into the adjoining stall, where, unluckily for Larry, an undercover cop lurked. To the public, in a news conference, the penitent yet fighting Republican, who voted against gay rights, proclaims in self-defense: "I regret the decision to plead guilty and the sadness that decision has brought on my wife, family, friends, staff, and fellow Idahoans. . . . Let me be clear. I am not gay. I never have been gay." Though not gay, he admits that the scandal has humiliated his constituency: "Through my action I have brought a cloud over Idaho." I am trying to picture that cloud. I am trying to picture the people on whom that cloud casts a shadow. On the police interrogation tape, post-arrest, he tells the persistent cop, "You solicited me. . . . Did our feet come together? Apparently they did bump." Asked to explain how their feet bumped, Craig tries to justify himself: "I'm a fairly wide guy. . . . I tend to spread my legs when I lower my pants so they won't slide." I'm a fairly wide guy, I'm a horndog loser, I'm a man in the stocks, I'm forced by the police to air in public some humiliating tales of sexual conduct—statements that are not intrinsically humiliating, but that cast a cloud over Idaho. I'm always horrified when I see a person lacerated in public for lewd conduct—especially when the person won't admit that he had fun. Let me be clear. When Bill

Clinton's extramarital escapades hit the press, I quaked with vicarious shame and outrage that a mere blow job should rock the nation and that this forgivable president and his wife and daughter and Monica Lewinsky and everyone who knew and loved Monica Lewinsky should need to suffer in public and be seen by hypocritical viewers and pundits and senators as humiliated beasts. Whether the accused are politicians or priests or parking attendants, I don't like to see them humiliated by facing trial—either in court or in the media—for the behavior of their mouths, genitals, or anuses. If this book has an ulterior aim, however disreputable, here it is: I want to stand up for those who are publicly shamed for sexual conduct. I'm not talking about rapists, or adults who take advantage of children—though my heart is capable of breaking for the pedophile, too, when the accused pedophile is Michael Jackson, or even someone not as talented or famous as Michael Jackson, even someone unknown until the public airing of the alleged action. I can't make a hero out of Larry Craig, who, as legislator, malignly obstructed gay rights. (My disgraced triumvirate of politicians—Larry Craig, Eliot Spitzer, Bill Clinton—were pilloried as much for their hypocrisy as for their sexual errancy.) In Congress, Larry Craig was a rotten foe of civil rights, but when it comes to cruising, I stand by him: I deplore the public humiliation of a bum who looks for sex in public bathrooms. I'm glad I've never been arrested. I'm glad I haven't had to appear on TV, or in front of "my wife and kids," in a press conference, confessing to having sex in an airport bathroom, or a train station bathroom, or a university bathroom. I'm glad I'm not bringing a cloud over the state of Idaho. Sex in bathrooms isn't intrinsically humiliating— though it can sometimes feel, to those who dislike the atmosphere, a tad compromising, especially if the bathroom is unclean, the floor wet, the odor unpleasant, and especially if the fear that a policeman or whistle-blower will suddenly appear gives pause to the reckless adventurers and makes their encounters seem unwise or self-destructive; but whenever a defendant is forced to confess to lewd conduct, this scene of incrimination belongs to a dreadful continuum, a plague-parade of suffering, including the Tribunal of the Holy Office of the Inquisition and the trial of Oscar Wilde.

10.

And now, since I've mentioned that Eliot Spitzer's head looks to me like a penis, at least when he resigns his office as governor of New York for sleeping with a high-priced escort ($4,000)—I want to add to this book's litany of humiliations (all stacked up for the purpose of showing humiliation's universality, and showing that humiliation can metamorphose—if the sensation of "hitting the bottom" is fully experienced—into redemption) some details about my own penis and its proclivities. (Politics is not my turf. Nor is TV. Nor is jurisprudence, or history. My turf is my body, an encyclopedia of wishes I can't help but incarnate, and whose index lies between my legs.) Before I aim my argument in that direction, let me offer a general word about redemption.

11.

I believe, with Jean Genet, and Jesus Christ, and Oscar Wilde, and a few other martyrs and mystics and trouble-makers, that humiliation is a kiln through which the human soul passes, and where it receives burnishing, glazing, and consolidating. Humiliation cooks the spirit to a fine finish. (About the experience of servitude, the great Robert Walser wrote, in his 1907 novel *The Tanners*, "Strange, too, that you might nonetheless experience this state of affairs as a sort of refuge, a home.") Neither Walser nor I consider humiliation pleasant. But if it didn't contain a silver lining, I wouldn't be examining this dismal category of experience. If humiliation didn't have the potential (sometimes, in certain circumstances) to transfigure the person over whom it casts a noxious cloud, then I'd drop the subject, and write, instead, about something genuinely redemptive, like white wine.

12.

Penises have two tendencies. They rise. And they fall. First, I'll discuss the rise. Mine rises often, too often, especially when it should, for decency's sake, stay down. I became aware of unwanted arousal at an early age—five? six? seven?—when a bully made me take off my pants and run across his backyard. Coincidentally, whenever my pants came down, my dick stuck out. The bully asked, "Why is your penis big?" I answered, "It's only big when I pull down my pants." And I thought, *I can't wait until puberty, when boys compare endowments.* Through scuttlebutt I'd discovered that adolescent boys size up cocks in locker rooms. Maybe I'd heard about circle jerks, too.

In any case, I was not humiliated by my tumescence, when the bully pointed it out; instead, I was humiliated by racing across his backyard naked. As perverse reward for the race, I begged him to show me his mother's college graduation photo. (I'd seen it before, and wanted to see it again.) His mother, now a fat drunk, had once been a beauty who'd studied psychology at UC Berkeley. And so I endured the humiliating—and arousing—experience of stripping for the bully, to receive, as payment, the pleasure of seeing the magical photo of his mother before her descent into drink.

13.

This tendency to become erect when I strip in front of men has stuck with me. Which means I'm often afraid I'll be humiliated by becoming aroused in an inappropriate circumstance. Last year I saw a dermatologist because I wanted to get rid of a persistent pimple on my nose. The doctor, who had pictures of his newborn child on his desk, was a complete professional; he said, "Let's do a full body screening." I removed shirt and pants—but not my undershorts. Soon the moment of unveiling arrived: he said, "Lower your shorts." I complied. So far so good; my king-of-hearts remained obediently flaccid. To keep it under control, I summoned dire thoughts—starvation, surgery, electric chair. And then he said, "Pull up your scrotum so I can look underneath"; when I performed the revelation, I could feel the telltale quickening and stiffening. I closed my eyes to avoid assessing the full extent of my crime: a boner in the medical suite. Unmoved, the dermatologist finished checking the joystick region and told me to get dressed. The paradoxical aspect of becoming hard in the wrong situation is that the erection—which some sages might consider a symbol of power and happiness—suddenly becomes the mark of shame. The weenie grown big suddenly seems a compromising sign of a failure to be masculine, a failure to behave, a failure to be indifferent. I am humiliated by my penis's refusal to be blasé. Too eager, too conspicuously glad to be seen by another man, it erupts at these telltale moments with the humiliating outspokenness of a cyst.

14.

In the locker room, I get hard whether or not I'm attracted to the nearby naked guy. The mere fact that *he can see me* sends blood to my dumbly responsive organ. To survive P.E. in school, to ward off a woody, I inoculated myself with horrific fantasies (images from Elie Wiesel's *Night*, babies thrown into fires). When, as a kid, I saw photos of nude frolickers at Woodstock, I thought, *I'll never be a hippie, a streaker, or a campus radical. I'll never go naked in public—I'd get humiliatingly hard.* Not once have I gone skinny-dipping. Like the "ugly" woman in *The Swan*, the weeping woman who confesses that she bought a car with tinted windows because she didn't want to be seen, I avoid exposing a sizeable part of my nature.

15.

I haven't often been impotent—the very word horrifies me: *impotence!*—but there have been signal occurrences, such as the first time I slept with a straight man (my magic wand lost enthusiasm when his teeth abraded it) or the first time I tried to have sex with a woman (I could feel a cold breeze through her bedroom's open window). With women I was always nervous. I "succeeded" at the erection game more than I "failed," and yet the failures felt so eviscerating—they were such glimpses into my own nothingness, such appalling instances of sense-blockage and paralysis (suddenly I'd remember the war-wounded amputee in Dalton Trumbo's *Johnny Got His Gun*)—that I decided, after a few years of uptight sex with women (I came too quickly, among other errors of com-mission and omission), that God didn't intend me to be straight. Nor did God intend me to be a senator. Like it or lump it: my pride and my sense of "face" (of dignity, worth, presence) is wrapped up in my penis, and though I am humiliated when it expresses *too much face,* too much eagerness to say hello to the world, I have been more humiliated by those moments, earlier in life, when it lay dead in my lap like a discarded and nerveless sau-sage link.

CATHETER
(THE QUEEN OF TROY IS QUEEN NO LONGER)

1.

TV is a manure pond of humiliation, contaminating the viewer. Watching *American Idol,* I'm smeared with the feces of mediocrity, banality, cruelty. I'm befouled by the hurt expressions of the humiliated participants, the wannabes who can't sing. I'm bombed with *E. coli* by the smug, brutalizing comments of the sometime judges—Paula Abdul, Simon Cowell, and Randy Jackson. The most sadistic is handsome Simon Cowell, who dishes out criticism so cruel, it makes me want to kick him in the nuts. Here are some of the comments by Simon and company: "You are one of the worst singers I've ever heard in my life, and I'm not exaggerating." "Dude, you shouldn't ever be singing . . . that was horrific." "I would check my hearing if I were you." "There's not a song in the world you could sing." "If I were to say you were mediocre, it would be the biggest compliment you've ever been paid." "You are a terrible, terrible singer." "Nate, you're tone-deaf." "You could do a voice-over for a rat." "You have no charisma." Human dignity is degraded by the Cowell/Abdul/Jackson parade of cruel gibes. The show, *American Idol,* is broadcast to one hundred countries, including Estonia, Finland, Iran, Malaysia, Singapore, South Africa, and Vietnam. The program teaches its millions of viewers that denigration is a delight, that the road to stardom is paved with shame, that Americans love to make fun of strivers, and that mass entertainment—the supposedly consoling, cheerful sound of a TV playing all day long in the restaurant, the barbershop, the gym, the kitchen, the bedroom—is a Muzak of humiliation, women and men weeping as they learn that their voices are "amazingly dreadful." *American Idol* is not alone to blame for propagating humiliation; TV itself—its insistence on ubiquity and universality, its *Candid Camera* wish to confuse reality and televisuality, its *1984*-Big-Brother ambition to erase private space by beaming public space into the home's bosom, its Oral-Roberts-holy-roller quest to erase religious difference, its quasi-fascistic mandate to coat the brutalization of consciousness with a business-as-usual, duty-obeying face—TV itself, with its newscasters and emcees, its brightness and flatness, seems humiliation's handmaiden, its spy, its mole, its emissary, its virus.

2.

And yet TV consoled me when I was a kid. I was addicted to *I Love Lucy*, *The Mary Tyler Moore Show*, *Bewitched*, *The Addams Family*, *Dialing for Dollars*, *Jeopardy!* *The Newlywed Game*, *The Dating Game*, *The Partridge Family*, *The Monkees*, *Dragnet*, *The Mothers-in-Law*, *The Patty Duke Show*, *Rowan & Martin's Laugh-In*, and *Longstreet*, which ran but briefly (its hero was a blind detective). But TV, its giddy, tacky, high-pitched, laugh-tracked patter, like a pacifier, or an electric blanket, or a space heater, or any other form of *fake bonding, fake comfort, fake nourishment*, greeted my desire for comfort with a measly substitute, a formulaic, pap-thin simulacrum. I wanted recognition; I got, instead, *Jeopardy!* And therefore I make TV my little monster. I demonize TV—I have avoided watching it for thirty-four years—because its episodic mediocrity can humiliate, even if there is not a Simon Cowell on the air to embody the humiliation by saying, "You're terrible." I scapegoat TV for reinforcing my own sense of humiliated isolation, disembodiment, and unfitness. I don't hold a grudge against the couch I sat on while watching TV. But I hold a grudge against TV. Superstitiously I blame the messenger. In the pre-1976 era of my boob-tube addiction, I felt beyond the reach of companionship (I watched *The Bob Newhart Show* instead of going to parties), and so I jumped to this melodramatic conclusion: *the TV-watching body has turned away from the spectacle of real life. Seeking consolation in TV, I'm doomed to occupy the position of shame-dweller, manure-pond-denizen.*

3.

A book, like a TV, drains me of my wishes and fears. I hook myself up to the book—the book I'm reading, the book I'm writing—and out pour the fluids I no longer want. Afterward, I feel sickened by my release, but also relieved; the toxins are gone, flushed out of my bloodstream. A book, for catharsis addicts, is a ritual chamber wherein we acknowledge that we are dirty and that we are capable of becoming clean.

4.

No stranger to dirt or to dirt's rituals, Jean Genet—homosexual, thief, writer—carved a pathway between sublimity and humiliation (life as orphan, life as thief, life as prisoner, life as faggot, life as devotee of his own filth, including his anus). Throughout his life and work he honed this connection between idealization and denigration, and it would be tedious to lead you through the details. I'd rather summarize, and say (paraphrasing the master) that Genet found God in his bowels. In *The Thief's Journal,* he mused: "The army, police stations and their hosts, prisons, a looted apartment, the soul of the forest, the soul of a river (the threat—reproach or complicity of their presence at night) and, increasingly, every event I have witnessed, create in me the same sensation of disgust and fear which leads me to think that the idea of God is something I harbor in my bowels." And by discovering God there, by locating redemption and transfiguration and immortality in the site of shame, he could fearlessly pontificate about the intrinsic beauty and worthiness of categories that most people consider foul. He felt himself humiliated by society, and by the men he desired, tough guys (convicts, pimps) who could only be brutal; he turned this humiliation into a proud desire to humiliate others, and into a prose style, an idiom of transformations and gildings, of metaphorical embroideries and rapid reversals of hierarchies (God/bowels), that gave him a permanent berth in an unstable universe. Style—forged from humiliation—unlocked the tabernacle. Genet found degradation sexually arousing—which isn't the same as saying he was a masochist. He considered humiliation aphrodisiacal because it was a necessary fact of life, and existence itself, in its plurality and perversity, aroused wonder in him. Blossoms and prisoners, he believed, were similar; at the beginning of *The Thief's Journal,* he claims, with axiomatic definitiveness, *"there is a close relationship between flowers and convicts. The fragility and delicacy of the former are of the same nature as the brutal insensitivity of the latter."* In a pithy footnote, he adds: "My excitement is the oscillation from one to the other." Oscillate from God to bowels, from flower to convict, and thereby experience pleasure not in one pole or the other, but in the dizzying flight between antipodes. Such rapid transit brings on the humiliation shiver, the puzzling simultaneity of ice and fire—a sensation that rushes, in the instant of humiliation, up and down my spine. We're back to T. S. Eliot, his still point of the turning (burning) world, his "crowned knot of fire," as he put it at the end of "Little Gidding." It was poor nerdy pale Tom Eliot, after all, who wrote, in *The Cocktail Party:* "I have had quite enough humiliation / Lately, to bring me to the point / At which humiliation ceases to humiliate." That is my goal: to reach the point of happy anesthesia, of indifference, where humiliation loses its foulness, or finds in its foulness a new, cocktail-bright divinity.

5.

But let's skip T. S. Eliot and get back to the sexier Jean Genet. I won't spend much longer on him, but I want to make sure you understand the principle he represents: *although humiliation hurts, it is an oblique pathway to transcendence.* Transcendence might be the wrong word. Perhaps I mean *the cessation of suffering.* Or maybe humiliation is the only indubitable, rock-solid truth that Genet ever found, and so he clung to it. But nothing I've said can explain the powerful intangibility and change-ability that humiliation offered Genet: a chance to occupy the ever-whirling turnstile of intensified consciousness, where inside and outside cease to differ. In *The Thief's Journal,* Genet rhapsodically summarized his creed: "This almost gleeful rushing into the most humiliating situations is perhaps still motivated by my childhood imagination which invented for me . . . castles, parks peopled with guards rather than with statues, wedding gowns, bereavements and nuptials, and later on, though just a trifle later, when these reveries were thwarted to the extreme, to the point of exhaustion in a life of wretchedness, by reformatories, by prisons, by thefts, insults, prostitution, I quite naturally adorned my real situation as a man (but first as a humiliated child whom knowledge of prisons was to gratify to the full) with these objects of my desire, these ornaments (and the rare diction pertaining to them) which graced my mental habits." If I use fancy language, if I depend on metaphors and complicated sentences, if I aestheticize any crud that crosses my path, if I behave antisocially, if I speak in unpopular and confusing ways, if I have sex in public restrooms, if I write, whenever possible, about having sex in public restrooms, if I repeatedly bring up "manure ponds" for the weird pleasure of saying "manure ponds," that is because I want to reject the world that has humiliated me, and because I ineluctably (and gleefully) rush into humiliating situations with the faith that abreaction is always possible. In *Beyond the Pleasure Principle,* Freud argued that we enjoy watching others get humiliated, or we ourselves rush to repeat humiliating situations, even if only in playful and un-serious reenactments, without consequences, because of the sense of psychic release—the cessation of pain—that repetition brings. When we watch a character humili-ated on stage or screen (Gloucester, his eyes jabbed out by King Lear's daughter; or Hecuba, once the queen of Troy, now become a slave, her "head shaved to the very bone"), we might experience joy: as Freud observes, "The artistic play and artistic imitation carried out by adults . . . do not spare the spectators (for instance, in tragedy) the most painful experiences and can yet be felt by them as highly enjoyable." Children's play, like the inventions of artists and writers, permit the player to dwell again in the intolerable region of humiliation, but this time encircled by the protective girdle of make-believe: "It is clear that in their play children repeat everything that has made a great impression on them in real life, and that in doing so they abreact the strength of the impression and, as one might put it, make themselves master of the situation." I'm not sure Freud is correct about abreaction: Genet, for example, didn't dilute the strength of his early humiliation; he simply performed an act of alchemy on it. Abreaction neutralizes value; al-chemy adds value. Alchemy is imaginative and moral transformation—or, as Nietzsche put it, transvaluation. Genet turns moral values inside out by repeatedly erotiz-ing the humiliated position—spit, stink, sperm. "Poverty made us erect," Genet, ever the masculinist, asserts. "In his solitary eroticism the leper consoles himself and hymns his disease." This book I'm now writing is a hymn to humiliation, and it is a somewhat phallic song, for which I hope you'll forgive me. In a counterintuitive detour, Genet's love songs to humiliation and filth circle back, tenderly, to the figure of the mother. (Perhaps because Genet's mother humiliated him by abandoning him, seven months after his birth, to a foundling home? Or because it is in relation to our mothers—and fathers— that we first experience the humiliation of existing in a helpless body?) Genet can "smile tenderly at the humblest among the dregs, whether human or material, including vomit, including the saliva I let drool on my mother's face, including your excrement." Always we loop back to excrement, which is not, in the symbolic chain that Genet and other criminal-lyricists construct, far from the mother's face, the first gaze, which honors but also humiliates.

6.

Many years ago, in the twentieth century, I found myself occasionally at a train station in the state of Massachusetts, during the great years when Edward Kennedy was senator; and the men's room at this train station, I noted, boasted a significant degree of erotic traffic. In that restroom, the most humiliating spectacle I confronted—and I confronted it repeatedly—was a guy in a wheelchair parked in front of a urinal for a long time. He never urinated. He had a catheter. He'd perch at the urinal, and if there were other guys jerking off at the other urinals, he'd watch, but never participate. Once, I stood at the far right urinal, while he sat parked at the far left. In vain, we both waited for someone else—someone sexy—to arrive. Together we waited; I snubbed the guy in the wheelchair, and he snubbed me. Cruising men regularly snub each other. The rejections are silent but humiliating. *(You're a troll. I'm waiting for someone better-looking. You're not my type.)* This man in a wheelchair was, I think, not white, though beyond *not white* I can't remember exactly what he was. But this part remains clear: he looked defeated.

7.

I'll tell the story again. In a men's room, I snubbed a guy in a wheelchair. He was parked by a urinal, though urination was clearly not his business. He hadn't unzipped his pants; he patiently sat waiting for a gentleman caller. I felt humiliated by his presence: the two of us waited, together, for the same dubious reward, which our sacred forefather called the kindness of strangers. The purpose of this anecdote, repeated, is to indicate the regular humiliation undergone by the disabled and the regular humiliation undergone by anyone with a complicated erotic agenda—and every erotic agenda, I'd wager, is complicated. I wonder what the guy in the wheelchair thought of me. He might have hooked up his catheter to the urinal for drainage. I can't remember much of the scene. But this part is indelible: I looked him directly in the eye and expressed no recognition of his worth or his presence. I expressed no recognition that I would ever consider him sexually eligible. And it is possible that he looked me directly in the eye and pronounced me equally ineligible. We both waited for someone else, someone worthwhile. The restroom stank.

8.

Ted Kennedy humiliated himself verbally at least twice, according to his obituary in the U.K. *Guardian*. With admiration and a predictable amount of Kennedy idolatry I followed Ted's political career, and I don't remember the verbal humiliations, though the *Guardian*'s obituary damned his 1980 presidential campaign as "a disaster from the outset," and claimed that "he was completely incoherent when asked why he wanted to be president." I've watched TV footage of Kennedy's response to the question "Why do you want to be president?" and I wouldn't call his hesitation "incoherent." However, it's evident that his performance (contradictory, evasive, rambling) was considered what we call in Yiddish a *shanda*—a scandal, a shame on the family. A nervous speech becomes incised in the historical record, through the obituary's tar-and-feathering, as "incoherent." Kennedy made a far more humiliating speech in 1969, after Mary Jo Kopechne's death-by-drowning. With the measured, stunned voice of the contrite sinner, the senator said: "And so I ask you tonight, the people of Massachusetts, to think this through with me; in facing this decision. . . . I seek your prayers." Should he resign? Will he be able to put this accident—which he calls, in a gesture of unfortunate understatement and euphemism, "this tragic incident"—behind him? "This last week has been an agonizing one for me and for the members of my family, and the grief we feel over the loss of a wonderful friend will remain with us the rest of our lives." He calls the death "these events." I'm not faulting him for his

tone or his statement or his actions. But I'm noticing
that the spectacle of a humiliation—or this kind of *political male humiliation*—involves a grave tone of voice,
a statesman's reasonable, numb, abstract voice, and that
this muted tone (and the lurid, or tragic, events it con-
ceals) becomes a kind of pornography. Powerful men
saying mea culpa, even in a neutral, deadened voice, give
me shivers of horror and identification: I recognize the
numbness and I recognize the culpability and I recognize the pornography of *a man in the stocks,* a man strung
up for our laughter and accusations and opinions, our
mutilating mockery. In 1994, after "a rape case in which
his nephew was eventually acquitted," the *Guardian*
obituary tells us that Kennedy "felt obliged to make a
humiliating public statement about his abysmal personal
life." Kennedy said, "I recognize my own shortcomings,
the faults in the conduct of my private life." I recognize
these recognition scenes: when the reckoning happens
in public, and in the theatrical medium of a television
interview or a televised statement, we are in the territory
of what Aristotle called *anagnorisis* (the sudden discov-
ery of one's identity, one's predicament). Now, on TV, in
the mouths of politicians or aspiring stars, the admis-
sions are public. Anyone can be Hecuba, formerly queen
of Troy, now slave with shorn head, crying out (in Alan
Shapiro's translation of Euripides' *Trojan Women*),
"Weep for me, / Trojan women, / Weep for this wretched /
Fate. I am gone. / The worst of all / Possible lots is
mine." She may be miserable, but she gets the audience's
attention. To her crazy child she cries out, "Cassandra, my
daughter, you breathed your inspiration / From the gods,

but now on what humiliating / Bed will you have lost your purity?" I'm commiting a few intellectual crimes. I'm conflating humiliated politicians with martyred Greek tragic heroines. I'm slipping between incommensurable categories. But I love to slip, and I have a noble aim: to urge you to be kind when you see someone humiliated, even if you think that the shamed person deserves punishment. Hecuba and Ted Kennedy are both obliged to moan in public, whether in passionate verse or in deadpan politico-speak, but neither Hebuca nor Ted Kennedy is happy to be forced to make a statement like "The Troy before you is no longer Troy, / The queen of Troy is queen no longer." I'm not Ted Kennedy, I'm not Mary Jo Kopechne, I'm not Hecuba, I'm not the guy in a wheelchair in a men's room in Boston, Massachusetts. And I'm not a tribal Kurdish daughter who will be murdered because I have been (according to *The New York Times*) "perceived to have dishonored" my family; I'm not a tribal Kurdish daughter murdered by my family in what they call an "honor killing," a ritual act that helps "cleanse their shame." We're all in the business of cleansing ourselves of shame. Some of us do it via TV. Our catheters are hooked to the remote control.

DISGUSTING ALLEGATIONS

1.

Maybe I'm drawn to write about the humiliation of Alec Baldwin because I find—found—him sexually attractive. Alec Baldwin, hunky movie star, left a nasty message on his daughter Ireland's voice mail. Someone leaked the message to the media; millions heard it. Millions heard him rant against Ireland for not picking up the phone when he called. For prurience's sake, and for the pleasure of passively repeating a sexy star's stolen words, I'll sample his diatribe: "I've made an ass of myself trying to get to a phone to call you at a specific time. . . . And you don't even have that goddamned phone turned on. . . . I'm tired of playing this game with you. I'm leaving this message with you to tell you you have insulted me for the last time. . . . I don't give a damn that you're twelve years old, or eleven years old, or that you're a child, or that your mother is a thoughtless pain in the ass. . . . You have humiliated me for the last time with this phone. . . . You've made me feel like shit; and you've made me feel like a fool, over and over and over again, and this crap you pull on me with this goddamn phone situation that you would never dream of doing to your mother. . . . I'm going to get on a plane . . . and I'm going to straighten your ass out when I see you." He called her "a rude little pig." He repeated the insult: "a rude, thoughtless little pig." Later, he made a public apology, in an interview with Barbara Walters, who, as far as I can judge from my limited, TV-phobic exposure to her technique, specializes in acting sympathetic toward people she leads into booby traps. In self-defense, Alec said that the tabloid journalists who publish dirt about stars (including private phone messages that no one but his daughter should have heard) are themselves living "with shameful secrets" and "make it their career to humiliate you." Whether or not it's true that we media whores are "filled with self-hatred and shame," the public humiliation of Alec Baldwin (caught in the act of denouncing his daughter, the "rude pig") leaves me in my usual, queasy position, watching a man's downfall, and wondering why I agree to occupy this role, rather than to refuse it by vowing to ignore the tabloid trade of trashing the stars.

2.

Harriet Jacobs describes—in her nineteenth-century autobiography, published in 1861 under the title *Incidents in the Life of a Slave Girl: Written by Herself*—the daily, wretched humiliations undergone by an enslaved African American. Harriet knows that a master's "authority and importance would be best established and maintained by cruelty," and so "nothing could please her [the master's wife] better than to see me humbled and trampled upon." Sexually harassed by her master, she nonetheless defied him; when she has a sexual relationship with another man, "a white unmarried gentleman," not her master, and becomes pregnant, she feels even more humiliated by her "fallen woman" status than she had by her "slave" status. "Pity me," she begs the presumably "virtuous reader" (as if all readers were virtuous): "You never knew what it is to be a slave; to be entirely unprotected by law or custom; to have the laws reduce you to the condition of a chattel, entirely subject to the will of another." The condition of being chattel, however, she does not label with the word "humiliation"; that term she reserves for the loss of her sexual honor ("The painful and humiliating memory will haunt me to my dying day"). When she declares to her master, "In a few months I shall be a mother," she loses her self-respect, and confesses to the unbesmirched reader: "And now, how humiliated I felt!" No mere semantic fussiness inspires me to point out that the word "humiliate" appears in Jacobs's book primarily in contexts of sexual dishonor; humiliation's wound impinges directly on the body's intimate parts. Humiliation shoves the inside outside, and the outside inside, by dragging forward into the public eye a private knot of suffering, vulnerability, desire, and corporeality. At that moment, the victim knows the sick, upchucking sensation of inner matter thrust outward, as the grotesque substratum of one's body (whether raped and disenfranchised, or vituperative and entitled) leaks and spews. It's not my place to speak for Harriet Jacobs, who writes her own story under the name Linda Brent. It's no one's place to speak for Harriet Jacobs, persecuted and articulate. When she turns fifteen (she calls that threshold "a sad epoch in the life of a slave girl"), the sexual torture begins: "My master began to whisper foul words in my ear." Verbally raped, she retains enough inwardness and self-awareness to measure the void that humiliation leaves behind as its nearly unspeakable trace: "I know that some are too much brutalized by slavery to feel the humiliation of their position; but many slaves feel it most acutely, and shrink from the memory of it. I cannot tell how much I suffered in the presence of these wrongs, nor how I am still pained by the retrospect." She cannot tell the full story. Acute feeling produces a shrinking away from the ability to describe it. It's difficult to know what Harriet Jacobs really felt; her words point toward that void but can never fill it. We can't even know whether sexual dishonor is the injury she felt most keenly, or whether the sentimental conventions in which Jacobs framed her autobiography demanded that the assault on her sexual propriety be given special treatment in the litany of terrors. It might not be rhetorically or ethically justifiable to have switched the subject, as I did recently, from Alec Baldwin to Harriet Jacobs, as if their situations were comparable. Perhaps I wanted to reestablish the dignity of the word "humiliation" by reminding myself, and reminding you, virtuous reader, that there have been brutalizations, in American history, beyond the slings and arrows aimed, by what Alec Baldwin calls the "tabloid media," at ranting stars, stars who remain worthy of our sympathy, especially when their private lives are unfairly broadcast.

3.

Michael Jackson talks to the media (*60 Minutes*) about the brutality he suffered at the hands of the L.A. police, and his shattering narrative leads me down the garden path of fascination and terror, as if I were overhearing an unspeakable procedure that I will never be able to explain or translate to the authorities beyond the valley of the gulag that Michael and I share for the duration of his account, a narration shorter than the trauma it unveils: "They did it to try and belittle me, to try to take away my pride. . . . They manhandled me very roughly. . . . With the handcuffs . . . they tied them too tight behind my back . . . in a certain position knowing that it's going to hurt. . . . One time I asked to use the restroom and they said, 'Sure, it's right around the corner there.' . . . They locked me in there for like forty-five minutes. There was doo-doo or feces thrown all over the walls, the floor, the ceiling. And it stunk so bad. Then one of the policemen came by the window, and he made a sarcastic remark. He said, 'Smell—does it smell good enough for you in there? How do you like the smell? Is it good?' and I simply said, 'It's alright, it's OK.'" And, if you are as appalled as I am by Michael's ordeal, and by the ordeal that a star's public statement itself entails, please listen closely and sympathetically to his 1993 statement, in which he refers to the charges of child molestation leveled at him, and to the police investigations of his body, an experience he calls "horrifying": "There have been many disgusting statements made recently concerning allegations of improper conduct on my part. These statements about me are totally false. . . . I have been forced to submit to a dehumanizing and humiliating examination by the Santa Barbara County Sheriff's Department and the Los Angeles Police Department earlier this week. They served a search warrant on me which allowed them to view and photograph my body, including my penis, my buttocks, my lower torso, thighs, and any other area that they wanted. They were supposedly looking for any discolorations, spotting, blotches or other evidence of a skin-color disorder called vitiligo. . . . It was the most humiliating ordeal of my life, one that no person should ever have to suffer; and even after experiencing the indignity of this search, the parties involved were still not satisfied. They wanted to take even more pictures. It was a nightmare, a horrifying nightmare. . . ." Forgive me for quoting abject stars. I like to hear—and memorialize, by repeating—every word they say in self-defense and self-incrimination, if only because of my nearly anthropological infatuation with the peculiarities of starry speech, its exaggerations and simplifications, its delicate dance between baroque grandiosity and cut-rate ordinariness, its position on the uncanny cusp between candor and prevarication. Michael Jackson's life, as it imploded in this moment of public testimony, reveals several layers of humiliation, which deserve enumeration. (1) Michael Jackson is accused of humiliating children by sleeping with them. (2) He is humiliated by the media, which enable and broadcast his statements. (3) He is humiliated by the police, who shackle, examine, and photograph his body, and confine him in a stinking bathroom. (4) Long before his arrest, he humiliated himself by undergoing extensive (and arguably disfiguring) plastic surgery. (5) Even earlier, in childhood, he was humiliated by his father, who beat him: as critic Margo Jefferson observes in her illuminating book *On Michael Jackson,* when one of the Jackson boys "missed a dance step, he got whipped—and mocked, and scornfully compared to whichever brothers hadn't messed up." Being humiliated by the police, and then humiliating himself in public testimony, echoes earlier degradations. (6) Michael, when young, was humiliated by media companies that turned him into entertainment. Being a child star is not a treat; it is a form of abuse, in which we, as spectators, as entertained audience, are complicit. As Jefferson argues, "Child stars have to live out adult mythologies. They work for adults. They perform 'youth' as scripted by adults and they work adult hours to do so." Michael Jackson may have been accused of "improper conduct" with children; but what about our improper conduct with Michael Jackson— what about the erotic and musical delight that his performances produced in viewers and listeners? Jefferson makes our complicity clear: "We talk about how we think, believe, suspect Michael Jackson treats children. We don't talk about how *we* treat child stars. Child stars are abused by the culture." I'd add: child stars are humiliated by the culture. Spectators pretend to exalt the kiddie wonder, but our exaltation erodes as easily as fingernail polish. Every little Shirley Temple is a casualty, a trough for abuse, including the abusiveness of too much fake affection and identification thrust in her unprepared face. And Michael Jackson, until the day of his death, at fifty (the same age Gloria Swanson was when she made *Sunset Boulevard,* whose final close-up exalted and humiliated her transparently needy face), remained a child star.

4.

Michael Jackson had much cause to compare notes on the humiliations of child stardom with his pals Elizabeth Taylor and Liza Minnelli. Liza, in particular, is a fulcrum of my curiosity about humiliated celebrities. I experience a complicated love for Liza when she appears on *Larry King Live* (I find these clips on YouTube, my shame-kiln) and speaks as if through a liquored bronchial prism, her voice luxuriously phlegmy and chortly, more laugh than speech. Mere quotations can't reproduce the grain of her voice, its occupancy of pleasurable interstices between word and cry. "Ah! [Chortle.] What are you talking with me about Elizabeth Taylor for! [Laugh] . . . I remember that when I went to Betty Ford, I called Elizabeth Taylor up and said 'They're saying I'm this and they're saying I'm that and dah, dah, dah.' And she said, 'Are you reading that?' And I said, 'Yes.' She said, 'Don't read it!'" Laugh, laugh, snort, laugh, chortle. The interview is glorious, a comic triumph tinged with mortification. She seems smashed. Liza Minnelli is not really humiliated; she just seems endearingly, embarrassingly uncomposed for the camera, too loose and sloppy in her locutions, too earthy, too untrimmed. It would be an exaggeration to call Liza Minnelli humiliated, but to such exaggerations I am prone; the alloyed pleasure I experience in seeing Liza acting loopy and inappropriate and overenthusiastic and unconscious of the boundaries of normal behavior comes from my assumption that she is humiliated and that the profession of "star" demands passage through shame. And certainly she might have considered it a monsoon of humiliation when her ex-husband David Gest publicly claimed—in the divorce trial—that she beat him up when drunk (she hit him so violently, he alleged, that he "sustained severe injuries about the head"). I'll never know if she is actually drunk on *Larry King Live* or if she has merely adopted the mannerisms of drunks and turned them into her own brand of grandeur and histrionics, a theatricality that compels the audience to shower her with love. When I heard her sing live at New York's Palace Theatre in 2008, she frequently told the vociferously enthusiastic audience how much she loved us, as if we were her mother. And I felt like her mother—or I felt cast in the role of her mother, her father—admiring Liza, cheering her on, trying to make sure she didn't humiliate herself by singing badly. I couldn't help being moved by the spectacle of Liza risking error and flaw and vulgarity, a humiliation she took as her origin and ground, as ever-present danger, as atmosphere and nourishment. Of course she didn't want to fail. But she knew that humiliation was the shadow of every song.

5.

Liza is what Margo Jefferson (in discussing Michael Jackson and other child stars) called an "archaeological site," containing "layers of show-business history." Liza contains Judy; Liza's woundedness is a response to her past, but it is also the very sign of the past, returned, as vibrato and appetite-for-applause, in a living body. The humiliations Judy underwent (called "my little hunchback" by producer Louis B. Mayer) continue in Liza's performances and more urgently in the unscripted media appearances (talk shows, interviews) that are her finest forum and stage. By appearing blasted on *Larry King Live,* Liza speaks Judy's humiliations and speaks the humiliation of being Judy's daughter, a daughter who can never express publicly her rage at the ruin that was her mother. (Would you have liked to be Judy Garland's daughter?) Performance culture—the demand to be a "hit"—is a sickness; performing badly is the cure. When an entertainer performs badly, as Liza sometimes does (or, to put it more accurately, when an entertainer performs irregularly, ill-reputedly, irresponsibly, incoherently, with an uncorrected rawness that a more conventional actor might find humiliating), such an artist commits a necessary, corrective aggression against the entire system of performance—a glass-menagerie system of false-self pas de deux that humiliates its stars and its audiences by placing both parties in fixed, untenable positions as collaborators in unhappiness. Liza spews out the fake love ("That's entertainment!") that she herself once swallowed from Judy; we, addicted to the entertainment drug, swallow it, in turn. We are bound together, star and spectator, in a symbiotic bond of mutual terror—Liza, humiliated by our defection, disappearance, disloyalty; we, humiliated by facing Liza's ruin; Liza, humiliated by needing to reembody Judy and carry forward Mama's afterlife, a soggy torch; and we, humiliated by feeling within our own bodies, in our gorges and intestines, a sick kind of love, groundless, based also on unacknowledged aggression, ours and hers. Liza has reason to be furious. And so do we. Watching Liza triumph and then crash, crash and then triumph, we witness humiliation's fiery presence within the mother-daughter bond. The poet Adrienne Rich wrote, in *Of Woman Born,* about a daughter's experience of beholding her mother's powerlessness under patriarchy: "Many daughters live in rage at their mothers for having accepted, too readily and passively, 'whatever comes.' A mother's victimization does not merely humiliate her, it mutilates the daughter who watches her for clues as to what it means to be a woman. Like the traditional foot-bound Chinese woman, she passes on her own affliction." Please forgive the audacity of this comparison: if we consider Judy Garland the foot-bound woman, who passes on to her daughter this message of what it means to be a woman, then imagine Liza's "mutilation" at being Judy's daughter, and imagine our humiliation, as we watch Liza and imagine ourselves to be the *third generation* of foot-bound star. As we watch her sing "New York, New York" again and again (even as we cheer, even as we shiver with uncanny pleasure), Liza passes on to us the bodily message of what it means to be a star. It might mean grandeur and money and luxury and ease, but it might also mean showing your buttocks to the Santa Barbara County sheriff and then going on TV to tell the world about the experience. It might mean a mansion in Bel Air, but it might also mean imprisonment by the L.A. Police Department for forty-five minutes in a bathroom smeared with doo-doo. It might mean private planes and Harry Winston jewels, but it also might mean delirium tremens at the Betty Ford Center, and garish caricatures of yourself in the minds of others. Not always garish: in many hearts, there are genuine shrines to the fallen star, shrines tended without irony, and without unkindness.

6.

I have made several attempts to integrate the following fact into a paragraph about Liza Minnelli, but I have not

been successful. Indeed, the attempt to integrate the following fact into a discussion of Liza might easily be characterized, by a witness, as obscene. Liza's humiliation—if
we call it that—has nothing in common with the nightmare experienced by a prisoner in Guantánamo, a man
named Mohammed al-Qahtani, who, according to the
Senate Armed Services Committee (reported by *The New
York Times,* December 17, 2008), "had been threatened
with military dogs, deprived of sleep for weeks, stripped
naked and made to wear a leash and perform dog tricks."
The interrogative technique, the *Times* tells us, is known
as "pride and ego down," from the U.S. Army Field Man-
ual on Interrogation (FM 34-52): the technique's purpose
(writes the *Times)* is to use "humiliation to try to over-
come a person's resistance." There is no need to integrate
this awful fact into a paragraph about a star's downfall
and rise; we are, however, burdened with a consciousness
that can be aware, simultaneously, of different levels of
suffering, from the mild to the unspeakable, a progres-
sion we can't call a continuum, although the same human body contains the dreadful potential for every
variety of "dog trick."

7.

I enjoy looking at porn, mostly gay male, especially when
the model looks directly in the viewer's eyes. Sometimes I see embarrassment or indifference in the model's gaze. Sometimes I see excitement or pride. Of course
the emotions I attribute to him are my projections.
Usually I imagine that he is superior to me (his body is
sexy enough to deserve exhibition); however, I favor

images marketed as amateur porn, featuring "real" men, men with appendicitis scars and unshaved chests, men without conspicuously developed muscles, men who seem partly ineligible for the camera's attentions. Looking into a model's eyes, I'm glad to have caught him in a direct confrontation. He has no choice but to meet my glance. But what if the model feels, at the time or later, years after the photo shoot, humiliated by the exposure? What if the photo came from a private session, not meant for Internet circulation? What if the model cooperated only because he was drunk or drugged or incapacitated, and later regretted his lapse in judgment? You could argue that the porn model is an "object" that I am humiliating, and that his humiliation contributes to the pleasure I take in porn. Whatever my motives, I have grown attached, of late, to a website called NewYork StraightMen.com. Whether or not the men are really New Yorkers and really straight, I can imagine that they are straight men who needed money and so agreed to take off their clothes and engage in acts that some straight men might find humiliating or unpleasant. (The work isn't arduous. These models—like the "rough trade" of an earlier era of homosexual history—receive blow jobs while murmuring taciturn, stereotyped exclamations; no one expects rough trade to reciprocate.) When the New York Straight Man, in a photograph, looks directly in my eyes, a specific parable unfurls in my body. I imagine that I've caught him in a compromised moment; I've "bested him"—or wrested from him a confession of subordination and vulnerability. He must acknowledge my desire. He can't resent, judge, or ignore it. He can't moralize it out of existence. He must surrender to its suchness, its factuality. I have "fucked" him—forced him to concur with my hapless, unimpeachable hunger—by looking at him when he didn't entirely want to be looked at.

8.

On another website, HunksWorld, I've found a video and photo sets of my favorite model, a guy who passes into public notice under the name of Ben Dodge. I won't bore you with a detailed description of his body (suffice it to say, he looks like a bellicose Alec Baldwin, with bigger lips and thicker eyebrows). I doubt that his real name is Ben Dodge. Another website, Hairy Studs Video, identifies him as Esteban, and calls him a "straight Latino bull"—a "businessman in Argentina by day" who "gets off on being filmed." The virtue of Esteban/Ben Dodge's performances, in stills or in moving pictures, is his readiness to look directly at the camera with a belligerent, sullen expression. I have grown to feel friendly and loyal toward him; I feel kindly toward him because he has given me a pleasure I must classify as vicarious because it happens in my body but is not entirely *of* my body. Nor is the pleasure my property. It is Ben Dodge's property. And to some extent I am (at least fantasmatically) humiliated by Ben Dodge, whoever he is, because this visible stranger is, in my estimation, more desirable, and therefore more real, more embodied, more material, than I am. Compared to Ben Dodge, I am abstract, ghostly, suppositional. Humiliation, in the world I share with Ben Dodge, happens at least twice. First, it happens to me: I've been humiliated by Ben Dodge because I depend on his image to help me occupy my desire rather than dwell at a distance from it. Ben Dodge brings me back home, to my better self, or to a self whose avidities have been activated. And yet—here is humiliation's second occurrence—Ben Dodge is someone I've humiliated. I've humiliated him by watching him repeatedly and by dragging him into my imaginative system. As, I suppose, I've humiliated Liza by dragging her into my interpretive system, and by demanding that she embody the mother-child knot of rage and paralysis, a sensation (or a lack of sensation) that I may never be able to put into words, not because it is too complicated, but because it is too simple, as elemental as the fact that I've humiliated Ben Dodge by harnessing him to my fantasies.

9.

I'll go one step further. On a level that may be entirely imaginary, I've humiliated someone else—a specific man, once my student—by enjoying pictures of Ben Dodge. Ben Dodge excites me not merely because of his own appearance, but because *he reminds me of someone else.* Ben Dodge reminds me of my former pupil—a sweet, smart, straight guy (late twenties? early thirties?) with a gift for subversion. I'll call him Eddie, in honor of the late crooner Eddie Fisher, a swoon-worthy Jewish star who humiliated Debbie Reynolds by dropping her for Liz Taylor, and who then was humiliated by Liz, in turn, when she dropped him for Richard Burton. When I look into Ben Dodge's eyes, I pretend, sometimes, that I'm looking into Eddie's eyes—and I imagine that I've exposed his double life. I've discovered that Eddie, my straight student, has a secret life as a nude model on the Internet. In Argentina, to boot! My straight student, Eddie, looks directly at me as he prepares for orgasm. My straight student, Eddie, slightly shuts his eyes when he comes—and this for me is the most poignant moment, when Ben Dodge, or Esteban, or Eddie, shuts his eyes, because he can't bear the intensity of an on-camera climax. It is too compromising, too absolute a plunge into the void. But then I start to feel sorry for my student, because I've dragged him onto the Internet; I've turned him into my prop. I've hijacked poor Eddie, my straight student, into becoming Ben Dodge. These are psychological, internal events—not actual. But they feel like tangible cataclysms, pageants. I have humiliated Eddie by seeing him naked, and he, reciprocally, has humiliated me by being sexually inaccessible—he's straight, and he's my student, and therefore off-limits. I was not infatuated with Eddie; but when I discovered Ben Dodge, I noticed that he reminded me of Eddie, and I fell in love with Ben Dodge, a phantom on the Internet, a series of photos, a video called *Latino Bull Jerking Off.* It is no accident that I am humiliating myself by telling this story to you, virtuous reader, *mon semblable,* you rude, thoughtless pig. That is the price of writing this book. I need to incriminate myself, to establish my bona fides as a humiliation expert. I learned these tricks from my mother, Judy Garland. One day I found her in the bathroom, pouring aspirin down the toilet. "Mama!" I cried. "Don't kill yourself!" I love you, Larry King, you rude pig. Thanks for asking me to appear on your show.

FINE JEW LINEN

1.

Elisabeth Schwarzkopf's master classes: I can't get enough of them. Earlier, hypocritically, I said that TV was a manure pond, and I pretended to be immune to its toxic charms. And now watch me jump again into YouTube, a manure rivulet, where, amid dreck, I find the inspiring master classes of the punitive German soprano Schwarzkopf, known by her catty fans as Betty Blackhead, and famous not only for her sterling voice but for her Nazi Party membership and her later denial of it. In master classes, she imposes lofty, draconian, mirthless standards on her pupils, and enacts a dynamic of discipline-and-punish unequaled in the annals of twentieth-century vocal culture. I, whose palms sweat with anxiety when I go to the opera (I'm nervous that the singers will crack a note or suffer a memory lapse), paradoxically love watching Schwarzkopf's strict inculcations.

2.

She objects to the audible "h." A student singer emphasizes the "h" in a song's words, and Schwarzkopf urges him to silence it: "We're all guilty of 'h's' in our time," she says, "but most of us have learned to eliminate them." Schwarzkopf's vocal hygiene demands that we eliminate the "h." On the tapes I've seen, from master classes she gave in 1980 in Edinburgh, the singers always gamely comply with Schwarzkopf's demands; but the absolutism of her rules, and their metaphorical connection to eugenic policies of elimination, purgation, and purity, give me pause. A singer who produces an audible "h" is a beast to be punished, shunned, corrected. A singer who nods, for emphasis, while singing, is liable to scapegoating. Schwarzkopf asks, "Can you do that without giving a bump of your head? I don't know why this happens. Many Americans do it. . . . It gets very tiresome. Don't bump the head. Everybody's doing it all the time, it's not only you. In England it's much less even than it is in America. I've never seen it outside those two countries. I have nothing against those two countries, but they bump their heads in order to make a point, all the time. We do it while speaking, but I hope we don't do it while singing." I see my own culpable mediocrity—every aesthetic mistake I've made—mirrored in the stunned, ingratiating face of the masterclass student, who will never be as accomplished or renowned as Schwarzkopf. This student, this guinea pig, guilty of audible "h's" and head bumping and wandering intonation ("And in tune, if possible!" interjects Schwarzkopf) and failure to crescendo ("Did I get my crescendo? It was intended, but I didn't get it")—this disciple smiles at the instructor, whose critical comments aim to satisfy and impress the gladiatorial audience.

3.

Mixed motives: I listen to classical music because I want to hear the culture of humiliation turned into beauty—I want to hear echoes of the *eliminated "h,"* reverberations of elements deemed unworthy of existence. In the perfected musical phrase, we can detect traces of the abject student—anyone qualifies for this position—who feared committing errors, who feared reneging on a required crescendo.

4.

Schwarzkopf's essence: taking pride in coldheartedly eliminating the "h." *I could choose to be softhearted and kind. But that would be a luxury that a Kommandant can't afford. I must shut off my weakness so that I can forthrightly eliminate the "h." It would be easier to pamper the "h," to mollify and coddle the "h," to feed the "h" its Cream of Wheat. But I must slay the "h."*

5.

Here is one of the reasons that Hitler rose successfully to power, according to sociologist Tilman Allert, whose book *The Hitler Salute* analyzes the "Heil Hitler" greeting, the compulsory hand-movement that brought the Führer's presence into every social encounter, even between friends and family: Hitler ascended because of "the general expectation that the charismatic Führer would reverse Germany's national humiliation," a drubbing that followed from "Germany's defeat in World War I and the punitive terms of the Treaty of Versailles." A perception that Germany had been humiliated led the downcast nation to transform itself into a machine that humiliated and murdered millions.

6.

Giorgio Agamben, in *Remnants of Auschwitz: The Witness and the Archive,* reminds us that we who did not "know the camps"—we who were not present— nonetheless exist in a shamed relation toward them: the shame of the survivor. Agamben analyzes Primo Levi's description of a soccer match that took place on a "'work' break" in Auschwitz, a game "between the SS and the representatives of the *Sonderkommando*," the "group of deportees responsible for managing the gas chambers and crematoria. Their task was to lead naked prisoners to their death in the gas chambers and maintain order among them." These guards then played soccer with the SS. Agamben argues that their soccer match is not a "brief pause of humanity in the middle of an infinite horror," but a continuation or intensification of that horror. And we, not present at Auschwitz, nonetheless feel shame: we feel "the shame of those who did not know the camps and yet, without knowing how, are spectators of that match, which repeats itself in every match in our stadiums, in every television broadcast, in the normalcy of everyday life." I feel shame not merely when hearing news of atrocity, but when hearing of leisure activities— music, entertainment—occuring amid atrocity and in its wake. It is possible to feel shame for actions we have never ourselves committed. When Harriet Jacobs, in *Incidents in the Life of a Slave Girl,* mentions taking a carriage, in New York, to Sullivan Street, I feel shame for Sullivan Street, a beautiful street in New York, a street I've walked with pleasure many times; I feel shame for Sullivan Street Bakery and the Sullivan Street entrance to the subway. I feel shame for my immunity to suffering, for my easy life. I feel shame for not being shackled, for not being slaughtered.

7.

Nudity is humiliating—or, to use the gentler word, shameful—because, according to philosopher Emmanuel Levinas, we experience, in this moment of nudity (especially, I'd add, forced nudity), a sensation of "being chained to oneself, the radical impossibility of fleeing oneself to hide oneself from oneself. . . . Nudity is shameful when it is the obviousness of our Being, of its final intimacy." Agamben extends Levinas's analysis of shame to include disgust, and quotes Walter Benjamin: "The horror that stirs deep in man is an obscure awareness that in him something lives so akin to the animal that it might be recognized." I'm afraid that you will recognize my disgusting bestial nature. I have already recognized it. My recognition horrifies me because I can therefore predict yours; I can foresee that you will shun and humiliate me.

8.

In Freud's famous essay "A Child Is Being Beaten," he analyzes his patients' recurrent memories of other children being beaten. Apparently, these analysands rarely remember themselves as victims of punishment, which lands on others. Freud notices that "the beaten child is never the fantasizing child, but regularly another child, generally a little brother or sister if there is one." And it is also possible for the scene of beating to flower into a variety of other humiliating situations, including vocal master classes. Freud: "The original simple and monotonous situation of being beaten can experience the most diverse changes and embellishments, and beating itself can be replaced by other kinds of punishment and humiliation." Beneath the fantasy of being beaten, or of watching someone else being beaten, lies, at times, an unconscious fantasy of being loved: "I am being beaten by my father" covers an original, repressed fantasy—"*I am loved by my father.*"

9.

I've tried repeatedly to write about the experience I consider the model for all humiliations I've seen or endured. This scene—my own version of *a child is being beaten*—dominates my imagination with an obscure power, a combination of horror and fascination, that I can never adequately put to rest. My language becomes anesthetized—as if reflecting a mind going numb—whenever I try to write about this scene, which I sometimes call, for shorthand, *kid with his pants pulled down in third grade.* When I was in third grade, my teacher punished a student—a boy named Bobby—by forcing him to pull his pants down in front of the class. She paddled his naked rear end with a paddle that always hung in a warning position near the drinking fountain. I don't know whether corporal punishment was legal in California, or whether this teacher was playing by her own rules. I know that I was afraid of this teacher, Mrs. H. I will call her Mrs. H., in honor of the "h," which Schwarzkopf demanded remain inaudible. The scene frightened and fascinated me for numberless reasons. (1) We could see the punished boy's penis. (2) He had pimples—boils?—on his buttocks. (3) He was crying: tears seemed as humiliating as nudity. (4) I was afraid that I would be the teacher's next victim. (5) The punished boy was not a good student; therefore I deduced that culpable academic performance led inexorably to genital exposure and buttock redness. (6) The punished boy came from a "bad" (wrong-side-of-the-tracks?) family, a dynasty of delinquents: seen from my milquetoast point of view, his tough brothers had criminal tendencies.

10.

I still haven't conveyed—or exorcised—the scene's power: though the boy was ostensibly the humiliated party, the teacher herself seemed humiliated as well, because she had forgone the dignity of her calling; she had involved herself in the boy's penis by exposing it; she had dragged the class into a turgid, low zone that I associate with fetid air, tuberculosis, mumps, nuclear fallout, soot, and a bouquet of other undesirables. It's possible, too, that I wanted to see the boy punished. It's possible that I felt relieved not to be the punished one. It's possible that I was riveted by the sight of his penis or his buttocks. My female classmates, too, could see his penis: *being seen by girls* seemed humiliating because, in my askew Weltanschauung, girls were not supposed to be aware of penises, and I imagined that if a boy could not keep his privates hidden, he had lost everything that made him potentially loveable. If a boy was not entitled to keep his dick away from view, then he had been dragged down to the level of a dog. When I reconstruct this incident, I see his genitals from the point of view of the Mormon girl who was an excellent student but whom I accidentally hit over the head, the year before, with a plastic chair. This Mormon girl, I hypothesized, would be especially shocked and shamed by the sight of the delinquent kid's penis.

11.

The scene tore my thinking mind into parts.

12.

The pimples on the punished boy's buttocks: I might be conflating two pairs of buttocks I saw that year. I might be confusing Bobby's butt pimples with the butt pimples of Randy, who lived at the far end of my block: once, playing at his house, I suggested that he pull down his pants. In the bathroom, he complied. I was shocked to discover that his butt was pimply. Shortly before or after that episode, his mother died. Therefore I firmly associate *pimples on a boy's butt* with *death of a boy's mother*. Next door to Randy-of-the-pimpled-ass lived a girl named Ann Taylor. Her last name, "Taylor," amused me because it seemed embarrassingly similar to "Toilet." *Ann Toilet,* I thought to myself, chuckling. How could she survive the shame of bearing such a name?

13.

As I watch the Elisabeth Schwarzkopf master class, 1980, I notice her big dress—almost a caftan. It seems designed to hide the body. I can't help imagining Schwarzkopf's hips, buttocks, genitals, and stomach underneath the gown; I wonder if she ever found her body to be a cause of humiliation. Notice my inability to stop imagining people's nude bodies under their clothes: any daydreamer can rely on imagination as a vehicle that apotheosizes as well as punishes. Agamben, in *Remnants of Auschwitz,* connects the experience of shame with the peculiar tendency of poets to erase their own subjectivities under the guise of intensifying them. Referring to John Keats, Agamben claims that "desubjectification"— becoming no one—is a "shameful and yet inevitable" part of poetic experience. And, quoting the Austrian poet Ingeborg Bachmann, who died after (accidentally?) setting fire to her apartment, Agamben attests to the connection between madness and this humiliating (or exalting) experience of being torn apart or rendered null, an act of self-erasure that is either blissful (Isolde enjoyed drinking her love potion) or annihilating (after too much self-erasure, the speaking ego disappears): "Bachmann claims that poets are precisely those who 'make the "I" into the ground of their experiments, or who have made themselves into the experimental ground of the "I."' This is why they 'continually run the risk of going mad' and not knowing what they say." I run this risk. I am experimenting on myself—trying to exalt and eliminate certain memories of humiliation, trying to exalt and eliminate the "nose" I have developed (like a hunting dog's) to catch the scent of humiliation. Tripping down the metaphoric chain in third grade, I connected the horror of seeing poor Bobby's paddled ass to the glimpse of the punitive teacher's breasts, visible, over her muumuu's top edge, when she bent down. Those revealed breasts—the authority of the vista—implied that she had *a right to know* the boy's butt pimples; she was the high priestess of demonstration, of exhibited skin, and she began her demonstrative career, in our classroom, with her own breasts, whose half-discerned shape I remember as not round but columnar. But now I'm guilty of turning her into an exhibit, and not even an accurately photographic one; in my rendering, she seems Cubist or Fauvist, distorted by surreptitiousness.

14.

Displaying one's humiliated status might involve pleasure or pride. The spanked receive the subtle reward of exhibiting their shame. At the root of the confessional act—whether in a poem or on a reality TV show—seems to be the pleasure, conscious or not, of publicly avowing one's misery, of showcasing one's lowered status, of turning the "loss of face" into a new face, a smashed, pulverized face, the face of the smacked, stunned, and vanquished. I may be humiliated, but because I am seen in the process of exhibiting my shame, I therefore gain *the pleasure of exemplarity.* To be exemplary—to be an example, a whipping boy, for the amusement of passersby—to be a placard, an admonitory parable—to be a star of suffering: Sylvia Plath, in her poem "Lady Lazarus," written in October 1962 (she committed suicide three months later), describes the circus pleasure of displaying her brocaded, gilt wish to be extinct. Boasting about an earlier suicide attempt, she says, "I rocked shut // As a seashell. They had to call and call / And pick the worms off me like sticky pearls." She is proud of those sticky pearls: they are her adornment, a sign of regality. Maggots may be crawling over her flesh, but she willfully transfigures shame into eminence, and decay into jewelry. Humiliation—or desubjectification, becoming mere animal, mere worm feast—becomes showmanship. (Or showwomanship.) A carnival attraction, like the Venus Hottentot, Sylvia's face is "a featureless, fine / Jew linen," a corpse turned back into houseware, usable, treasurable, worth displaying. The Venus Hottentot was Saartjie Baartman (1789–1815), an African woman enslaved and exhibited as a circus curiosity in Europe. Saartjie speaks, as if from the dead, in Elizabeth Alexander's poem "The Venus Hottentot": "I am a black cutout against / a captive blue sky, pivoting / nude so the paying audience / can view my naked buttocks." Plath controlled her own exhibition; any poet, however wild, controls and instigates her performances of captivity. And we may, as poets, wish to impersonate and imagine situations of extreme captivity for reasons that are not merely selfish; wanting to ask questions of horror, to know where it begins and how it might end, we may have a compulsion to touch, with respect and terror, the zero-degree instances of desubjectification that remind our fingers of the possibility of frost.

15.

I don't claim that Saartjie Baartman, forced to display her body, enjoyed the pleasure of exemplarity; that is not the direction in which I wish my argument to tend. There are circumstances in which the laws of pleasure and consolation, we can assume, cease to apply, and where desubjectification, to use Agamben's term, has operated with such ferocity and thoroughness that there may not be a recognizable subject left to experience any gleams of paradoxical reward. Nonetheless, there are figures who, in prison, have claimed to experience transfiguration; Oscar Wilde, exposed as homosexual in 1895, sentenced to prison and hard labor, claimed to have found in his humiliated circumstances a Christlike dignity. Just as there can be only one Jesus (but billions of Jesus-imitators), there can be only one Oscar Wilde, who, by following in Christ's footsteps, becomes the homosexual Bethlehem-baby. Whether Wilde actually experienced this transfiguration or faked it for literature's sake, he did a plausible job of impersonating a god; in a long letter from prison, posthumously published under the title *De Profundis,* Wilde glorifies his own suffering, or squeezes from it the lesson that by embracing his newfound humiliation, and accepting it as a necessary humility, he can forgive his enemies and attain equanimity. Wilde describes the worst day of his life, November 13, 1895, when he was exposed to the laughter of the mob: "From two o'clock till half-past two on that day I had to stand on the centre platform of Clapham Junction in convict dress, and handcuffed, for the world to look at. I had been taken out of the hospital ward without a moment's notice being given to me. Of all possible objects I was the most grotesque. When people saw me they laughed. Each train as it came up swelled the audience. . . . For half an hour I stood there in the grey November rain surrounded by a jeering mob. // For a year after that was done to me I wept every day at the same hour and for the same space of time." Ritually he revisits and rekindles the shock of his exposure. Toward what end? Toward salvation. The transfiguration, involving beauty (and therefore aestheticism), is not exactly religious, though he uses the language of piety: "So perhaps whatever beauty of life still remains to me is contained in some moment of surrender, abasement, and humiliation." He can't change his circumstances, so he must change the point of view he brings to his situation. He must change his interpretation of suffering. "What lies before me is my past. I have got to make myself look on that with different eyes, to make the world look on it with different eyes, to make God look on it with different eyes. This I cannot do by ignoring it, or slighting it, or praising it, or denying it. It is only to be done fully by accepting it as an inevitable part of the evolution of my life and character: by bowing my head to everything that I have suffered." Liza Minnelli could have said the same. *What lies before me is my past. I must bow down to Mama's death, I must bow down to the allegations, spread around the globe, that I beat my husband, David Gest, when I was drunk on vodka. I can't change what happened to me, but I can make the world look on it with different eyes. I must imitate Christ—the crucified Christ, not the headstrong, cheeky Christ who shunned his mother at the marriage in Cana.* The King James Bible renders his words as "Woman, what have I to do with thee?" Mary merely made a suggestion: she told him that the wedding guests wanted wine. "They have no wine," Mom said. And Jesus, sassy, replied, "Woman, what have I to do with thee?" Mary knows what it means to be humili-

ated by her son. That's why José Saramago, in his novel
The Gospel According to Jesus Christ, allows Mary to say,
sardonically, with the wisdom of a martyr: "You have to
be a woman to know what it means to live with God's
contempt." She was a Jewish mother. I'm stunned by the
rudeness of Jesus's rebuke, "Woman, what have I to do
with thee?" though I can imagine saying it to Elisabeth
Schwarzkopf if she tells me I haven't eliminated the "h"
from my singing or speaking, I haven't eliminated the
Homosexual, I haven't eliminated the stain of Hitler, I
haven't eliminated the memory of Mrs. H. paddling
third-grader Bobby's naked ass, I haven't eliminated
the Venus Hottentot's buttocks (as Elizabeth Alexander
writes, "In this newspaper lithograph / my buttocks are
shown swollen / and luminous as a planet"), I haven't
eliminated Humiliation as teaching tool, flash card, and
rallying cry. History hangs together in baffling clusters,
like swollen grapes, but without beauty, and without the
possibility of offering nourishment; the clusters may add
up to nothing but a command to remain curious about
the chance circumstances that led the awful episodes to
fall together into one moment in time, one moment of
remembrance or speculation. We have an obligation to
keep asking questions about experiences that are not our
own, experiences that are worse than our own will ever
be—or that is what we pray, we pray that our experience
will never grow so catastrophic as to encompass the lowest points in recorded history. (They fall together—these
nodes of experience, these leitmotifs—just as at the moment of death, I imagine, all particles of experience are
hurled together in a terrible storm; and they fall together

because there is nothing more basic to two human beings standing near each other than that one has the capacity to destroy or debase the other.) After Saartjie Baartman's death, her genitals, pickled, were exhibited in Paris at the Musée de l'Homme. They remained on view until 1974, the year that Michael Jackson, with the Jackson 5, performed in Africa for the first time.

SHOCK TREATMENT AESTHETICS

1.

My favorite humiliated artist and writer is Antonin Artaud (1896–1948), who received an abusive abundance of
electroshock treatment, and who experienced inspiration
as impregnation and rape from demons. As Anne Carson
put it, in her poem "TV Men: Artaud," "Some days he felt
uterine. Mind screwed into him by a thrust of sky." And
this invagination—Artaud, supposedly male, feeling himself uterine, penetrated by phallic sky—made him God's
bride, God's prostitute: "He felt God pulling him out
through his own cunt. Claque. Claque-dents." For years
I've murmured that odd word "claque-dents" as a private mantra signifying humiliation's potential for being
transformed (via aesthetics) into a chewable, repeatable
morsel, like a tobacco wad or a betel quid. A "claque-
dent," according to the notes for Clayton Eshleman and
Bernard Bador's translation of Artaud's final works
(*Watchfiends & Rack Screams),* is "a miserable wretch,
a brothel," or a "beggar." I'll repeat Carson's scandal-
ous line: "He felt God pulling him out through his
own cunt." God's cunt, or Artaud's? In either case, Artaud feels humiliated by God, though perhaps also honored. Carson—an astute reader and channeler of Artaud's
spirit, a spirit humiliated into artistry, as if misery were

the apprenticeship that permitted aesthetic flowering and accomplishment—writes (in her poem "The Glass Essay") of her own humiliated relation to sexuality. One lacerating outburst demonstrates Carson's Artaud-like willingness to make art directly out of her lowest moments: "When nude / I turned my back because he likes the back. / He moved onto me. // Everything I know about love and its necessities / I learned in that one moment / when I found myself // thrusting my little burning red backside like a baboon / at a man who no longer cherished me." Tell it to me, Anne! Which is more humiliating—the action, or its repetition in a poem? Carson becomes an artist—an Artaud—because she has the nerve to put her little burning red backside like a baboon into a poem that is nominally an essay. Carson isn't humiliated. She is elevated into the guild of the Claque-dents, the transvaluators, the art makers who feel that "mind" (its pointy penetration) is "screwed" into them like a dentist's drill. One memorable day in my early childhood, while perched on the toilet I imagined that my emerging turd was Satan, poking me from behind. I've never forgotten this sensation: Satan screwing himself into me. That experience helped me understand poetry and painting, those difficult, urgent arts.

2.

Claque-dents. Artaud had a rough time on the Catherine wheel of mental illness and its concomitant confinements. About Artaud's nearly nine years in "five insane asylums," Eshleman declares: "One of his acquaintances,

Jacques Prévert, said that what he went through was worse than deportation to a concentration camp." That might be an exaggeration. But it sets a certain mood: mind screwed into you. Here are the last words that Artaud wrote before dying of intestinal cancer: "And they have pushed me over / into death, / where I ceaselessly eat / cock / anus / and caca / at all my meals, / all those of THE CROSS." Like the Marquis de Sade and Christ, Artaud perceives himself at both the foul and the empyrean ends of the universe's seesaw. To eat cock, anus, and caca at all his meals is not fun; but he seems to brag about this cuisine. It makes him lordly. It makes him mortified. It makes him worthy of adulation and canonization.

3.

According to Eshleman, Artaud "received fifty-one electroshocks"; was "injured and terrified" by the treatment, which fractured his "ninth dorsal vertebra" and sent him into a ninety-minute coma ("three to four times longer than the typical coma following electroshock"); suffered "serious intestinal hemorrhages"; begged his doctor "to halt the treatment"; lost his teeth. Electroshock screwed its power into his body; mental illness and psychiatric treatment felt like God raping him. Artaud's work overflows with messianic accounts of psychic violation: in the poem "Artaud the Mômo" he writes, "**god** / sat down on the poet, / in order to sack the ingestion / of his lines, / like the head farts / that he wheedles out of him through his cunt." I can't resist one more excerpt from this oracular merde-fest: "in the

filth / of a paradise / whose first dupe on earth / was not
father nor mother / who diddled you in this den / but / I /
screwed into my madness."

4.

Phantoms from Artaud's imagination (like an intestine,
coiled yet pointed) ransacked and penetrated his consciousness, buggered him to death. He called this im-
molation "mysticism," an experience linked to punished
anality: in *Interjections,* he writes, "The extreme point of
mysticism, / I hold it now in the real and in my body, /
like a toilet broom." Mystical transport, to Artaud, felt
like being raped by a toilet broom; that's a metaphor.
What follows, however, is not a figure of speech: in 1997,
in a men's room, New York City police officer Justin
Volpe plunged the broken end of a broom into the rec-
tum of Abner Louima, a Haitian man, and then shoved
a toilet plunger into Louima's mouth. This case—along
with the 1991 beating of Rodney King, attacked by Los
Angeles policemen, an atrocity captured on videotape
and circulated in the media—brought home to a usually
inattentive public the routine brutalization of blacks by
police officers; the assault on Louima, and the image of
pain and humiliation that it lodged in the imagination
of any of the millions of people who heard or read about
it, is now as present a part of this historical environment
(the atmosphere around me, New York City, this welter
of interlocking bodies and edifices and institutions) as
nitrogen. Which is to say that anyone who breathes is
"thinking" about humiliation at every moment, whether

or not the thought takes flight. I've spent a long time
wondering what justifies invoking the assault on Louima
within the context of a discussion of Artaud's artwork,
and I've decided that there is no justification except the
fact that I live in New York City and I have seen what I
have seen and a toilet plunger repeatedly mentioned by
the newspaper of record as an instrument of rape will
not easily leave the conscience of a sane reader.

5.

The brutalizing effects of madness—and the punish-
ments meted out by doctors—unleashed Artaud's anar-
chic works. Neither Joan of Arc nor Abner Louima, but
subjected to a suffering described as if it pertained to
their martyred spectrum, Artaud brought a paranoid
style of prophetic exclamation to the task of uttering
what it felt like to be slaughtered by authorities, including by *one's own authoritarian tendencies.* Artaud, in a
series of late dictations, proclaimed: "And not like god, /
but like, being, me, / this unique body, / from where
all, / even god, came out, / that I have been violated for
life, / insulted, offended, dirtied, / polluted, muddied,
smutted / . . . that I have been a little bit everywhere mar-
tyrized." I identify with Artaud's description of writing
(or any act of art making) as torture, as a process of being humiliated by ideas, images, internal phantasms,
and external censors. Here is how Artaud characterized
the book *Interjections,* which includes those dirtied
dictations: a "type of book absolutely impossible to read, /
that no one has ever read from end to end, / not even its

author, / because it does not exist / but is the fruit of a consortium of incubi and succubi nailed, stabbed, planted everywhere, / pullulating, in the body of Man, / turned over and over like a turkey on the grill." Ouch! That is what it feels like to write: I'm nailed and buggered and stabbed by incubi and succubi. And each stab, each penetration, each pullulation, is a phrase I try to turn into a complete sentence. The process of making art—no party— has the atmosphere of an internal crucifixion.

6.

Jean-Michel Basquiat used written language in his paintings and drawings, and the presence of these words— often in block lettering, all capitals, like flash cards, explanations, signs, graffiti—evoke unpublished writing, writing on the fly, school-primer writing, hornbook writing, the use of alphabetic letters (A B C D E F G) to punish and instruct. The presence of written words, lists of them, crossed out, smudged, expresses a humiliated relation to literacy and language but also a triumphant, sardonic, playful appropriation of block lettering as a way to firework the punitive system. Every user of language must have experienced the distress of getting it wrong, and must have wanted, as an act of revenge and love, to humiliate language right back in the kisser. Every time Basquiat uses block lettering in his drawings and paintings, I imagine that he is humiliating language and expressing the ever-present possibility that language could reciprocate the harsh treatment. In the painting *CPRKR* (1982), Basquiat stacks up a list of words, surmounted by his

trademark crown: "STANHOPE HOTEL / APRIL SEC-
OND / NINETEEN FIFTY-THREE." He crosses out the
"THREE," replaces it with "FIVE." Claque-dents. Below,
the name "CHARLES THE FIRST. / .I" announces Charlie Parker's royalty.

Charlie Parker, martyr and genius, who died—of
drink?—at the Stanhope Hotel, receives canonization at

Basquiat's hands. In an untitled work on paper from 1981, Basquiat wrote "FAMOUS NEGRO / ATHLETES" under a crown; on another, he wrote "ORIGIN OF COTTON" above a black-line square, like a cube or box. In the drawing *Undiscovered Genius* (1982–1983), Basquiat plays with the word "Mississippi." He writes it five times, each attempt or reiteration stacked on top of the one before. In one, he circles the double "SS"; in another, he puts a red box around the "MISS" and a circle around the "PPI." He writes, twice, a list of foodstuffs, one item stacked above the other, the stacking itself a replication of how humiliation stacks up the feelings inside one's stomach and squeezes them hard together: "MEAT / FLOUR / SUGAR / ALCOHOL / TOBACCO / CORN." At the top of the drawing, beside the figure of a rudimentary Statue of Liberty, Basquiat draws the outline of a ship, which he labels "SLAVE SHIP©," the copyright symbol alerting us to the commodification of history and to Basquiat's own canny, adventurous adoption of African American history's originating humiliation as his own wily trademark, or as an item he can treat as a rudiment, a toy, an aesthetic building-block. In the painting *Hollywood Africans* (1983), he writes the phrase "Hollywood Africans" five times; twice, he crosses it out; once, he festoons it with the copyright logo. To cross out a word is to humiliate it; to cross out a word is to indicate, however obliquely, that *words have already crossed me out*. In the painting *Television and Cruelty to Animals* (1983), Basquiat writes "POPEYE VERSUS / THE NAZIS." but crosses out the "A"; and elsewhere on the same surface, he writes "POPEYE / VERSUS / LOS NA / ZIS," as if trying out a Spanish version of the slogan; but this time he crosses it out, as, at the bottom of the painting, he crosses out the words "VERY EXPENSIVE."

I receive intense, unmediated pleasure from Basquiat's emphatic lettering; he treats words as visual objects, and he converts a painting into a poetic text, reverberating with unparaphrasable significance. Basquiat seems to be humiliating the system of language; he also seems to be humiliating the viewer with these allusive, bewildering, yet comic verbal announcements. *Language is a system that has punished me; and so I, as reciprocation,*

will punish language. As with graffiti, which either communicates or confuses, depending on who is looking at it, Basquiat's use of lettering is a gauntlet he throws down, daring us to read him.

7.

Language as an orderly system, a set of codes, a discipline, puts to shame anyone who tries to step into its stronghold. And Basquiat's lettering—words placed, as if wrongly, in paintings and drawings, where we're surprised to find them—expresses shame and its transformative reversal into pride, anger, audacity, art. In the painting *Eroica II* (1988), a list of alphabetized slang words displays the abjectness of minority idiom but also its liveliness, beauty, intricacy, and intellectual subtlety: "BAG-PIPE" means "VACUUM CLEANER," "BALL & CHAIN" means "WIFE," "BANANA" means "ATTRACTIVE LIGHT SKIN BLACK FEMALE," "BANG" means "IN-JECTION OF NARCOTICS OR SEX," "BANK" means "TOILET," "BARK" means "HUMAN SKIN."

We learn these equivalences, these Baudelairean correspondences, every noun a symbol of another noun; we study them, master them. And we experience the graphic effect of Basquiat remastering them, rewriting them, emphatically and bluntly, in the style of a chalkboard pedagogical demonstration or of a billboard's commercial announcement, putting down words that sometimes put us down.

8.

Language hurts. Language humiliates. And not just when it's ungrammatical or unsanctioned. Language, as a system of displacements, substitutions, links, finessings, and crosswirings, fucks someone over. Someone is always being screwed by language. Bank means toilet. Ball & chain means wife. The words—sneers—deride their referents; the secrecy of language (whether the school-tongue of the oppressor, or the underground, graffiti-scat tongue of the oppressed) humiliates those who can't penetrate and decode its secrets, or those who are forced to live only in the holding pen of its incomprehensibility. It's humiliating to speak only in code, only in a punished, subaltern idiom; but it's humiliating to stand outside that vernacular, too, and not comprehend it, and feel its disrespect.

9.

As Basquiat jabs language by graffitiing it, and thereby expresses both a humiliated relation to language and an active desire to humiliate the pants off it (*fuck you, language, for ripping me off*) as well as to worship it (*words, you grand, sick creatures, you have stood above me, on your throne, for too long, and now I must crown myself the prince of the underworld text*), so Artaud, our man tied to the electroshock pallet, jabs language by making drawings that are also poems, artifacts that he calls "Spells," intended to cast hexes against enemies.

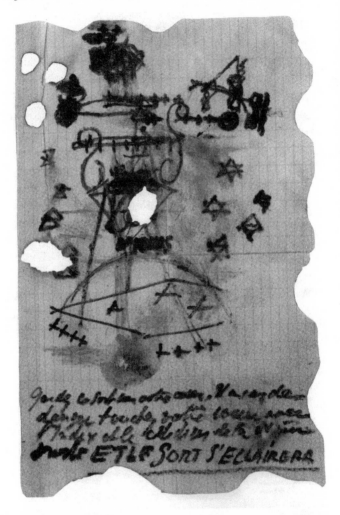

To complete the sadistic sorcery, Artaud set fire to the page itself—puncturing it with burn marks, whether with a match or a lit cigarette. These spells are horrifying documents—hardly recognizable as artworks or as poems, they look like crucified or tortured bodies, pocked with burns and holes, or like a combination of a Venetian lace curtain, a cave painting, and a fragment of Judaica salvaged from a burnt synagogue after a pogrom. I will be learning lessons from these spells—Artaud's magic, burnt pages—for the rest of my life. The holes he burned in them seem not to interrupt but to continue the words, as if literature aspired to the condition of a hole: the word wants to be a wound or to express a writer's wounded relation toward language, and so the inscribing hand must burn the page. These holes are the puncture points of meaning (Roland Barthes uses the word *punctum* to describe the "prick" of significance that jumps out from a photograph to seize the viewer's eye); Artaud's holes, the places where God has screwed him, the place where, as Carson phrased it, he "felt God pulling him out through his own cunt," are the most exciting spots in his demented, incendiary oeuvre. Like Basquiat's block-lettered words, Artaud's holes make an announcement—a grim yet excited ultimatum— that language, when seized by the dominated mind, must undo that domination with whatever acts of fire or puncture or orthographical literalness are required. Basquiat's words ("NEGROES / NEGROES / NEGROES," "MISSISSIPPI / MISSISSIPPI / MISSISSIPPI / MISSISSIPPI"), like Artaud's spells, repel ghosts. A Basquiat painting, *To Repel Ghosts* (1986), puts the letters "TM," for trademark, below the block letters "TOREPELGHOSTS," with almost no space between the words, as if words were more punished, more shamed, when shoved together than when

allowed to stand apart. And I seem to be shoving together all my ideas and inferences, as if to humiliate
them, or to prevent them from freely breathing.

10.

I turn now to the work of Glenn Ligon (a contemporary
painter and conceptual artist honored with a Whitney
Museum of American Art retrospective in 2011), whose

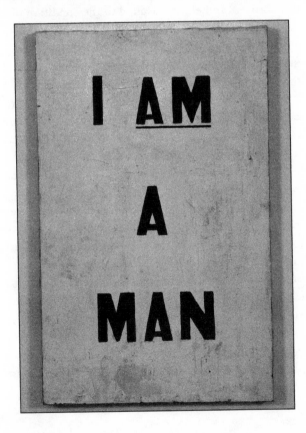

iconic painting *Untitled (I Am a Man)* (1988), a black-on-white oil-painted reproduction of a civil rights movement placard, confronts us with the polyvalent phrase "I *Am* a Man," the word "Am" underlined. Our eyes are caught between reading the bold, ambiguous words, and enjoying the white surface of the abstract background on which the words float. Ligon doubles the meaning of the initial historical utterance. The force with which the African American activist spoke against his dehumanization—I *am* a man—is intensified when Ligon asserts, twenty-five years after Martin Luther King, Jr., was imprisoned in Birmingham, Alabama, and nine years before the torture of Abner Louima, that manhood goes in many different directions, and that to say "I am a man" is not a transparently clear utterance. Am I really a man? Is it easy to know what a man is? Do I become a man just by saying, in an act of performance, that I am? If I fail to be recognizably virile, am I still a man? "I am an invisible man," Ligon declares in another painting, which retraces, in oil-stick letters, the first words of Ralph Ellison's novel. Has "I am" ever been an easy thing to say? The letters, in Ligon paintings, are stenciled, and thus they seem in thrall to a mind-numbing, rote, punitive apparatus, rather than to issue forth spontaneously as autobiographical words. Mediated, anesthetized by formalism, Ligon's borrowed words speak of humiliation (invisibility, unmanning) and simultaneously reverse it with their painstaking yet uneditorialized forthrightness, their insistence on being *merely words,* not images, not graphic depictions, not sentimental or authentic exhortations. Ligon's words are spells: they speak of harrowing classrooms, of learning to read, of failing to learn, of the punished threshold between literacy and illiteracy; and they speak of the retributive mechanisms of the adult artist, who "takes back the night" by marching, in block letters, stenciled or graffitied, pokerfaced or ranting, into your consciousness. The words in Ligon's paintings, however, are sometimes so thickly painted that the shape of the individual letters disappears, and the words become unreadable. "I FEEL MOST COLORED WHEN I AM THROWN / AGAINST A SHARP WHITE BACKGROUND," begins one Ligon painting, repeating Zora Neale Hurston's words, but as we scroll down the painting, reading it, the words grow obscured with paint; and as articulation becomes smudged and encrusted, we feel that the attempt to combat humiliation with fervent, soulful speech meets the deafening interruption of paint itself.

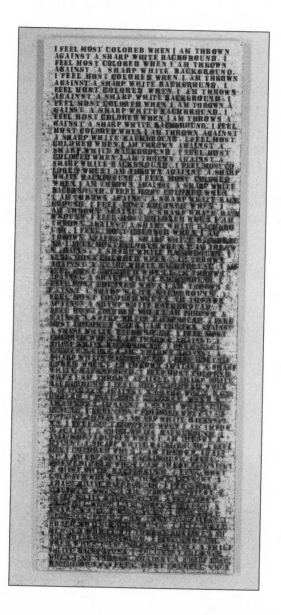

The medium erases the message. The medium humiliates the message. Thus (so goes the parable) is the artist humiliated by his or her materials.

11.

I understand that you may perceive I am exaggerating the links between words and humiliation in the art of Artaud, Basquiat, and Ligon; I can imagine that you consider my logic attenuated, my argument motivated by unarticulated agendas. There may be a certain justice in your claim. I am applying the word "humiliation" to works of art that use words—and holes, and crossings-out, and smudges—for a variety of purposes, and that make these ambiguous marks not to advertise abjection but (at least in Basquiat's and Ligon's works) to exercise self-possession, playfulness, and irony, and to advance an argument rooted in conceptual art's history. To counter the critique that, with good reason, you level at my logic, I can only suggest this modest rebuttal: I am a writer and it is in the supposedly "adult" and "safe" zone of writing that I feel most keenly the unpredictable and illogical incursions of humiliation as an *internal event*. And therefore I must talk about words. About words as objects. About erased, crossed-out, defiantly block-lettered words. About holes burnt into paper. After all, you are holding a book, composed of words, which emerged from my hands and my imagination with struggle, unwillingness, desperation, and nearly physical unhappiness, masquerading as catharsis. If you're not satisfied, virtuous reader, I invite you to light a match and burn a hole in this page. Become a book burner. Or copy my words, in block capital letters, on a page of your own. Become my amanuensis, my humiliated scribe.

12.

I've postponed the repayment of one debt, a deep one, owed to my late friend and colleague Eve Kosofsky Sedgwick, who pioneered the field of "shame studies," as some might call it, by writing several influential essays on shame's role in queer literature and culture. In one of these essays, "Shame, Theatricality, and Queer Performativity: Henry James's *The Art of the Novel*," Sedgwick memorably describes shame's power to undo boundaries between individuals: "Shame is both peculiarly contagious and peculiarly individuating. One of the strangest features of shame, but perhaps also the one that offers the most conceptual leverage for political projects, is the way bad treatment of someone else, bad treatment *by* someone else, someone else's embarrassment, stigma, debility, bad smell, or strange behavior, seemingly having nothing to do with me, can so readily flood me—assuming I'm a shame-prone person." If you are reading this sentence, then you are a shame-prone person. And the "shame-delineated place of identity," as Sedgwick calls it, or the nodes of "shame consciousness and shame creativity" (Genet and Artaud would have greeted with joy the phrase "shame creativity") "cluster intimately around lesbian and gay worldly spaces." She lists some of these arenas, in a litany that infuses a receptive reader with a vicarious spurt of energy and a sense of wonder that our modern world should so abound with possibilities for expressive efflorescence: "butch abjection, femmitude, leather, pride, SM, drag, musicality, fisting, attitude, zines, histronicism, asceticism, Snap! culture, diva worship, florid religiosity; in a word, *flaming*. And activism." Sedgwick found corroboration of her own shame-proneness in the theories of psychologist Silvan Tomkins, whose works she collected in *Shame and Its Sisters*. And though I'd differentiate shame from humiliation (shame is a flushed, abject feeling, while humiliation is the entire apparatus that causes the shame to erupt, the entire theater in which shame appears, a theater including torturer, victim, and witnesses), Tomkins links the two affects as one cluster: shame-humiliation. And he hinges his theory of shame-humiliation upon botched, thwarted encounters—moments when another person's strangeness, coldness, or unkindness interrupts one's own "interest or enjoyment." Shame arises when something happens that "reduces interest or the smile of enjoyment," and which then produces "the lowering of the head and eyes in shame" and prevents "further exploration or self-exposure." Tomkins's list of shame's possible triggers fetchingly centers on the note of "strangeness," the alien, the unfamiliar and the unrecognized: the shame affect might be triggered "because one is suddenly looked at by one who is strange, or because one wishes to look at or commune with another person but suddenly cannot because he is strange, or one expected him to be familiar but he suddenly appears unfamiliar, or one started to smile but found one was smiling at a stranger." Put it like this: if you don't want to read my book, or if you refuse to read me, or if you dislike this book I am offering to you as if it were a microcosm of my body for you to caress and inhabit and respect, then I will feel shame. Shame inheres in language. It is impossible to speak honestly without fearing the eruption of shame—an eruption caused by *your refusal to respond, to enjoy, to reciprocate, to reward, to greet.* In a passage Sedgwick admired for its comforting resemblance to Gertrude Stein's litanies, Tomkins genially wrote: "If I wish to hear your voice but you will not speak to me, I can feel shame. If I wish to speak to you but you will not listen, I am ashamed. If I would like us to have a conversation but you do not wish to converse, I can be shamed. If I would like to share my ideas, my aspirations, or my values with you but you do not reciprocate, I am ashamed. If I wish to talk and you wish to talk at the same time, I can become ashamed. If I want to tell you my ideas but you wish to tell me yours, I can become ashamed." The sign of shame is the bowed head: "The shame response is an act which reduces facial communication." My eyes and head drop, I wilt, I cease to look into your face. I cover my face to shield it against your shaming gaze. Getting excited can be humiliating, if you do not get excited in response to my excitement. Everything in this paragraph I learned from the eternally excited Eve Kosofsky Sedgwick. I would not be writing this book if she had not introduced shame as a sexy, redeeming, unbashful spot in contemporary intellectual life. Eve understood "shame creativity." She understood that without shame a writer might be deprived of the wish to write—but that sometimes shame could overwhelm and cripple the ability to get the words down. Hence my attraction

to Artaud's holes. In those burnt spots, I see the stig-
mata of his shame, a shadow that nearly cancels expressivity.

13.

In Eve's presence, I sometimes felt ashamed of not being
smart enough, or of being too forward, too comfortable,
too confident. Something shy in her bearing seemed to
cast doubt on the decency or efficacy of other people's
ease. Her shame, in other words, was contagious; trying
to describe her, I feel a double dose. She died of cancer
nine months before I began to write this book. The last
time we met, her legs were paralyzed. With pride and
wit, she referred to herself as a "full-fledged crip"—a
phrase of delighted identification with a minority group;
she said that she was curious about learning how to
navigate New York City without being able to walk. Thus
again she proved herself an expert at turning humiliation—or suffering, or depression—into an imaginative,
loving enterprise. She described herself, in person and
in print, as "fat," a word she didn't avoid. In an essay
(cowritten with Michael Moon) on John Waters's im-
mensely large and inspiring Divine, a drag performer
(originally named Glenn Milstead) who starred in *Pink
Flamingos* and *Multiple Maniacs* and other impolitely
visionary films, Sedgwick pointed out that Divine was
an apostle of "spoiled identity," and that Divine's spoil-
age created opportunities for other spoiled identities to
form a constellation around her; among this galaxy of
damaged eminences were "Jean Hill, a 400-pound black
woman, and the also huge Edith Massey, a gravel-voiced,

gap-toothed, radiantly magnetic, declamatory, and probably retarded older white woman." One kind of viewer might think that John Waters was humiliating Edith Massey by casting her in his movies. Another kind of viewer—I'm that kind, and so was Eve—understood that the act of making Edith a star, seeing her abjectness not as humiliating but as radiant and divine, came from the same universe of transvalued antipodes that made "Divine's obesity" not "unlovable and powerless" but "magnetically irresistible." Stigma becomes glory. Fat becomes beauty. I'll close this fugue with an affirmation of fat, and a shout of praise for Sedgwick's energizing gesture of what she called "coming out as a fat woman." She wrote, in a sentence that blasts apart any assumption that humiliation-destined people should be meek about claiming public space: "Denomination of oneself as a fat woman is a way . . . of making clear to the people around one that their cultural meanings will be, and will be heard as, assaultive and diminishing to the degree that they are not fat-affirmative." In other words, if you don't affirm the worthiness of fat, you're a fat basher.

14.

I loved Eve's wrists. They were large. Mine are small. That someone could potentially humiliate her by saying or thinking the word "fat"—this was a fact she seemed always to know. An image rises now before me of the jade bracelet she wore, a shallow sea-green circlet that Artaud might have recognized as a gris-gris, a spell against shame, a burning sensation in which she was proud (never a simple emotion, never remote from sadness) to bask.

15.

In Francis Ponge's prose poem *Soap,* a book whose strangeness intensifies the pleasure I take in it, he speaks of soap's disintegration in water as a form of humiliation: "The soap avenges itself for the humiliation it undergoes by intimately blending with the water." By confusing itself with water, by marrying the water, the soap discovers that "all memory of dirtiness dissolves." The soap forgets its shame. However, as a side effect, the soap suffers a loss of dignity: "lost face." "It finds itself seriously punished" for this loss of face. Death is humiliating because in its pond we disappear.

16.

"Unemployment is humiliation," says a piece of graffiti in Chile, February 2009. Big block letters, as if in a Basquiat painting: CESANTIA / ES HUMILLACION. In a photo printed in *The New York Times,* a man, his head bowed in shame, concentration, or distraction, walks by the sign, painted on a green wall. The man's shadow falls, as if in a noir melodrama, on the letters "MILL."

17.

Illiterate, deaf James Castle, who never learned sign language, became an artist (the kind called "outsider") and constructed small books, assembled from found paper; in these books—like visionary comix, or home-brew missals, or Emily Dickinson's fascicles—he borrowed alphabets without necessarily understanding them. (Not just books—Castle also copied words and letters in his paintings and collages. And sometimes, instead of reproducing actual letters, he invented simulacral, blurred, nonce alphabets.) The medium he used for art was humble: soot and his own saliva.

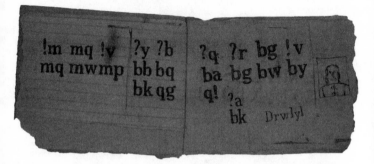

I wonder if James Castle ever felt humiliated because he was deaf and because he never learned sign language, never learned to lip-read, never learned to read. His parents ran a post office in Garden Valley, Idaho; correspondence arrived daily. He couldn't decipher words. But he loved them, as objects. He imitated them, in an act of patient, worshipful mimicry. The words he copied but couldn't understand were agents of humiliation, pressing down upon him; he pressed back, in tender retaliation. His relation to correspondence—to communication—to expressivity—was evolved yet stunted; shamed yet energetic. Patiently he put together his nonsense books. From spoiled identity, he gleaned rewards, silently. To the humiliated belong the spoils.

EAVESDROPPING ON ELIMINATION

1.

Humiliation is always personal, even when it lands on an individual because of group characteristics. A Nazi humiliates a Jew; the Jew takes it personally. (Am I wrongly extrapolating?) Humiliation's wounds are always intimate, pointed punctures. By moving outside my own experience, and trying to account, in however haphazard a fashion, for certain historical or cultural occurrences, I fear I've traveled too far from the solid terrain of my own humiliations. The only ground I can justify covering is also the country I most want to flee.

2.

The San Francisco avant-garde writer Dodie Bellamy, in her 2006 book *Academonia,* makes a list of her personal humiliations. Their candor excites me. The juiciest involves elementary school bathrooms: "I'm in first grade, sitting on the toilet, girls are peeing silently in the stalls on either side of me, but my pee is noisy, rushing against the side of the toilet like urine storm, I clench so it stops and try to let the urine out in dribbles so my peeing will be quiet as the other girls' peeing." Another resonant humiliation takes place at a poetry reading: "I've just finished reading at Cambridge, I'm freaked out by my cold reception, and then I look at my stomach in horror—my black pants are unzipped revealing a vivid white stripe of panties." Here, in emulation of Dodie Bellamy's list, I'll offer my own litany of small humiliations. None are major. None are life-threatening. None refer to the wretched of the earth. All are remediable. All refer to the ordinary progress of an ordinary life. Some are merely embarrassing, not humiliating. Some merely illustrate social awkwardness, or the shame I feel about my own unkindness. Making this list, I am torn between joy and disgust.

3.

At school in fourth grade, I sneezed: snot flew out my nose and mouth and onto my hands. I didn't know how to get rid of the gunk. I tried to wipe it on my pants and on the desk's underside. Everyone in the class—or so I imagined—could see my snot-smeared palm. Paralyzed, I waited for recess.

4.

Third grade: during a play rehearsal, a fellow chorister started trembling. Gradually a urine puddle encircled his feet. Worse than the urine was the trembling. A janitor mopped up the mess. The urinator quit the play.

5.

In a Buick station wagon my mother yelled at me in front of my debate partner, a girl with a perennial tan.

6.

Maybe listing the humiliations, one by one, is a futile strategy.

7.

I made a lunch date with my piano teacher. At the appointed time, I waited on the lawn outside her studio. An hour later, when she finally showed up, she seemed puzzled to see me. I asked, "Weren't we scheduled to have lunch today?" She said, "I'm very busy." That was the end of our encounter.

8.

A girl I wanted to "make out" with (she had big breasts) said, "Let me feel your biceps." I clenched my right fist. She felt my pseudo-bicep and laughed: "That's not a muscle," she said, and added, "I have bigger biceps than you do."

9.

When a barber finally cut my embarrassingly long and frizzy hair, a friend said, "Now that you have short hair, people won't mistake you for a girl."

10.

Sitting next to a playwright, I began ejaculating, and at just that instant an urban planner walked into the room. The playwright departed and left me in the room with the urban planner, who sat there looking at me, cum all over my hand. Every time I saw the urban planner, henceforth, I wondered whether he thought of me as "the flummoxed writer with cum all over his hand."

11.

My mother, choking on a piece of bread at a fancy restaurant, made ghastly sounds. Other customers looked disapprovingly at our table.

12.

My mother pulled a knife on my father, whose shocked aunt sat watching on a black leather chair. (The knife had a dull blade.)

13.

A plump-faced girl in seventh grade ran out of French class (I was standing in the hallway: why?) and fled to the bathroom. Brown shit streamed down her white stockings. Later, her obliging mother delivered a change of clothes to the school's front office.

14.

In seventh grade, a big kid hung me up, by my belt loop, on a doorstop.

15.

Bullies slammed my brother against gym lockers. My parents complained to the dean.

16.

At seventeen, I still hadn't learned how to drive: I'd opted out of driver's ed. Lying, I told a potential girlfriend that I had a license. A few weeks later, in her presence, my mother scolded me: "You need to get your driver's license!" The potential girlfriend snickered.

17.

My father told me that the redheaded lady who lived down the block was "ugly" and "plain." I imagined this woman's humiliated life.

18.

My father told me that my seventh-grade science teacher "couldn't spell." I defended the poor speller. I said, "He's not an English teacher!" My father persisted: "He's illiterate." I looked again at the mimeographed handout, an ecology flowchart with puerile misspellings.

19.

Recently I wrote a commissioned essay about a painter. The curator told me that the painter was upset by my essay and that it would be pulled from the catalog.

20.

Recently I wrote a commissioned essay about politics for a magazine. The editor told me, "Everyone here agrees that your piece won't fit in our issue."

21.

Recently I wrote a book review for a literary magazine. The editor called my essay a "botch" and didn't publish it.

22.

An acquaintance who worked for Random House told me, "I'm the reason that Random House rejected your book." He smiled. I pretended to consider his confession witty and piquant.

23.

I gave two of my poetry books, warmly inscribed, to a major poet. A few years later, my protégé told me that she'd found those very copies, with their embarrassingly effusive inscriptions, at a used-book store.

24.

At an academic conference, a student stood up, during the question-and-answer period, and accused me of assigning only white writers in a seminar he'd taken with me. Some audience members, apppreciating the student's bravery, applauded.

25.

After the panel ended, a colleague—whom I considered culturally conservative—came up to hug me. I told him not to hug me right now; I didn't want my revolutionary accusers to see me collaborating with privileged humanists.

26.

The next day, I called up this colleague and asked him out to lunch. At first he refused. He said, "You shunned me." The next day, at the café, he told me about a lifetime of being shunned.

27.

Later, this colleague died of AIDS. I didn't visit him in the hospital.

28.

A girlfriend wrote me dozens of letters, which I didn't answer. Whenever a new letter arrived, I felt humiliated by my negligence; and yet I knew I was humiliating her by not replying. The stack of letters (I saved them) proved my ingratitude, selfishness, sociopathology.

29.

An ex-girlfriend crawled into my bed. I was burning with fever. I said, "Go away. I'm sick." She said, "Please let me sleep here." I said, "No, go away." She continued to beg.

30.

A friend said that she had an episode of spontaneous, uncontrollable vomiting and diarrhea at the restaurant where she was a waitress. She lay on the bathroom floor, between door and toilet. A fellow waitress rescued her and cleaned up the filth.

31.

Reported by a friend: a guy at the gym wore skintight shorts. While he exercised, blood droplets seeped through the fabric in the back. Hemorrhoids? A trainer told him, "You're spotting."

32.

Seventh grade: one night I jerked off for hours without stopping. The next day, my swollen penis looked like a dreidel. Afraid that the swelling would never die down, I told my mother that I had an upset stomach and begged to stay home from school, lest I reveal, in P.E., my deformity.

33.

A young friend had a nervous breakdown and telephoned repeatedly from the mental hospital. He left phone messages ("Come visit me"); I never called back or visited. Was I humiliating him? Perhaps. But I also felt humiliated by my own refusal to respond generously to his distress.

34.

My sister adopted a stray cat, although my mother disapproved. The cat stayed in the garage, not in the house: that was the rule. One night by accident I let the pet leap into the kitchen. To shove the abject kitty back into the garage, I used a broom. Nagging question: can animals be humiliated? Or do they suffer pain without the stinging awareness of having been debased?

35.

My boyfriend is allergic to cats, but one night we "house-sat" in an apartment with a cat. We locked the animal in the bathroom so it wouldn't crawl into our bed. All night our victim cried and threw itself violently against the bathroom door. We cowered under the sheets; we feared that the cat would die of fright and sorrow.

36.

1977: a friend threw my pillow against a wall still wet with fresh paint. No sane reason motivated her gratuitous act of staining my pillow. (It was a throw pillow.)

37.

Out of the blue, this former friend, decades after staining my pillow, left two messages on my answering machine. I returned neither of them.

38.

Outside an elegant restaurant in Tribeca, on a bitterly cold winter night, a black man in shabby clothes said, "Merry Christmas," and asked for money. I was with three friends, all three not black; we hadn't yet eaten. One friend gave the beggar a dollar bill. Unsatisfied, the mendicant said, "I'm diabetic." I fished into the pockets of my leather pants and found three quarters, which I gave to him. He shook my hand. Instantly, I made a mental note to wash with soap before eating.

39.

A friend, raped in Rome, had a difficult time recovering. Her mother, who lived in Baltimore, flew to Rome and stayed with her in a fleabag apartment. They argued incessantly.

40.

Years later, this friend, white, married a black man. Some members of her family disapproved: one elderly relative allegedly said, "If only the groom were handsome, like Sidney Poitier."

41.

In seventh grade, when the history teacher explained the extermination of the Jews, a classmate, not Jewish, said, "Hitler was a smart cookie."

42.

If I hear a colleague poop loudly, in the school bathroom, I pity him. I feel that I am humiliating my colleague by eavesdropping on his elimination.

43.

I used to consider my father humiliated when he pooped in the bathroom, especially if I could smell it afterward.

44.

If I could smell my mother's poop, in the bathroom (she reserved her energies for the "master bathroom," though my father often availed himself of the "kids' bathroom," a less exclusive venue), I felt sorry for her, too, but not as sorry as I felt for my father when I could smell his production. A father's poop was more humiliating than a mother's. Poop captured the essence of a man's nature. Within my mythic system (to recount it here embarrasses me, but I must conquer the shame and accurately report my findings), poop mirrors masculinity, while poop contradicts femininity. Thus, if I become aware of a man's poop, I participate in his humiliation; but if I become aware of a woman's poop, I merely observe a case of mistaken identity.

45.

In Paris, on a freezing winter night, a woman squatted on the curb, pulled up her skirt, and let out a long curling turd. I stopped, startled by her shame. (I realize that I'm contradicting what I said above about poop and femininity.) When I stepped away from the horrid spectacle, a fellow passerby, who erroneously assumed that the defecating woman was my friend, accused me of abandoning her.

46.

On the Avenue of the Americas, in the 1980s, I saw a large woman stop in the middle of the sidewalk, spread her legs wide, release a torrent of urine, and then continue walking. (She was wearing a housedress.) Shameless, unbothered, she seemed a paragon of efficiency; she had figured out an easy way to handle the problem of elimination. And yet I could sense her action's ripple effect on every witness.

47.

In sixth grade, we were required to build a dodecahedron with plastic drinking straws. The teacher led us, step by step, through the process of assembly. But I stopped paying attention; my dodecahedron construction got waylaid. Days passed; I couldn't catch up. My classmates had completed their dodecahedrons; mine was a case of arrested development.

48.

I've told this story many times. Our eighth-grade English teacher assigned a book report: "Pick your own book, but make sure it's a classic," she said. I chose *Jane Eyre*. The teacher said, "No. That's a girl's book. Read a boy's book, like *Northwest Passage*." I rebelled. I stuck with *Jane Eyre*. The teacher asked every student to give an oral report—except me. She skipped me, though I'd prepared a hefty presentation. Perhaps the teacher wanted to spare me the humiliation of reporting on a girl's book.

49.

1969: a kid made fun of my high-pitched speaking voice.

50.

My best friend, in high school, criticized my smooth legs: "They look like chicken skin," he said, beside the swimming pool.

51.

A kid in seventh-grade gym, on the soccer field, called me a "wop faggot." I was flattered to be mistaken for an Italian.

52.

When I was in my late thirties, a distant cousin referred to me (behind my back) as "the Ritalin kid." (A neutral party reported the statement.) I've never taken Ritalin.

53.

When a graduate program turned down my application, the rejection letter began, "Dear Ms. Koestenbaum."

54.

An internist with a huge penis—we were both nude in the locker room—told me I had a flat ass.

55.

In sixth grade, because of behavioral problems (I talked "out of turn"), the teacher moved my desk to the front of the class, next to the blackboard, away from other students. My mother and father saw the conspicuous, punished position of my desk when they came to school for parent-teacher night.

56.

A violently negative review of my book started rolling out of my fax machine.

57.

Years later, a violently negative review of my book started rolling out of my fax machine.

58.

I threw away my fax machine.

59.

A prominent novelist, formerly a friendly acquaintance, stopped greeting me at parties. I deduced that she'd ceased to consider me worth cultivating.

60.

Boys in my high school gym class called me Woody. They thought I looked like Woody Allen. They didn't intend the comparison to be flattering.

61.

When Woody received negative press for his sexual relationship with Mia Farrow's daughter, I felt sorry for him. Ignoring Mia's angle, I thought only of poor Woody, humiliated by the media.

62.

At the airport recently, a man at the Delta ticket counter said, "You look like Woody Allen," a comment I decided to consider anti-Semitic.

63.

Riding my bike down a major street, I stopped at a traffic light beside a car whose driver and passengers were laughing, presumably at me.

64.

When strangers laugh in my vicinity, I assume myself to be the object of their mirth.

65.

I telephoned a cute girl named Becky, one Saturday afternoon in seventh grade, and asked her to "go steady." She laughed and said no. Immediately, I telephoned my second choice, Nancy, and asked her the same question. She, too, refused.

66.

One Saturday afternoon, when I was in seventh grade, an unknown party telephoned and asked me to participate in a survey about physical education. He wanted to know my weight and height; he asked how many push-ups I could do. I began to suspect that it was a crank call. Perhaps the caller was a classmate who'd seen my maladroitness in P.E.?

67.

Freshman year in college, a stranger telephoned my dorm room and asked, "Are you gay?" He cackled and hung up. I presumed he'd seen me cruising the glory holes at the library.

68.

In college, I applied to major in creative writing, an option limited to five students per year. At my interview, I said that I'd been influenced by Carl Jung's theory of archetypes. The department turned down my application.

69.

I came unprepared to a rehearsal of Schumann's D Minor Piano Trio. I couldn't play my part. The coach chewed me out for unprofessionalism.

70.

Instants before a performance began (I was accompanying a clarinetist in a Brahms sonata), my page turner whispered, "Someone who heard you practicing this afternoon said you 'banged.'" (Banging is a pianistic crime.) Unnerved, I stumbled during the opening phrase.

71.

Decades ago, I told my friend, a precociously successful writer, that I kept a diary. She said, "I write only for publication." We were watching a sunset together. I had published almost nothing. She had appeared in leading magazines.

72.

My father said to me, one morning in my adolescence, "You have bad breath."

73.

One of my favorite students confessed recently that when he was thirteen years old, he kneed his father in the balls—so strongly that the father passed out.

74.

This year, at the San Francisco airport, on Easter afternoon, while waiting on the security check-in line, I saw a grown man kick his pubescent daughter in the ass. She wore blue jeans; she had a maturing "figure," with full hips and breasts. I'd estimate that she was thirteen. Her father, white, spoke French; extremely handsome, he looked like Alain Delon or Paul Auster. (I'd chosen this security lane deliberately, among three other possibilities, because I wanted proximity to the sexy stranger.) The daughter immediately burst into tears, glared at her father, and turned away from him. A man standing behind me, a black man, said, "In Ghana, that's not the way a father treats a daughter." He pointed to his heart: "I feel it here." He said: "It makes me angry." Today, I reminded myself, was Easter, a day of paradigms. Until this moment, I hadn't noticed the man from Ghana, who was also handsome, though not, in my opinion, as eye-catching as the father who'd kicked his daughter. The man from Ghana, who looked like a businessman, wore a deep blue starched shirt. The French father had long sideburns, and reminded me of Vittorio Gassman. Earlier I said he looked like Alain Delon and Paul Auster. In fact, the French father looked like many different famous attractive men. He wasn't standing behind his daughter when he kicked her. He was standing next to her. His leg pivoted athletically and vigorously toward the right, like a judo kick, or an unconscious reflex of retaliation and self-protection. *I see my daughter misbehave. Ergo, I kick her ass.* The gesture—the sideways kick—seemed accustomed, formulaic, a gesture he'd perfected. The girl's face turned red, a combination of rage, blushing, and tears. She looked remorsefully at her father, whose expression didn't thaw. The mother, impassive, ignored the scene. She said nothing, did nothing. She, too, was good-looking, but not as good-looking as her husband or her daughter. The man from Ghana and I continued to commiserate—mostly through silent, shocked glances at each other—about what we'd seen. I felt guilty for considering the abusive father attractive. I felt consoled by the presence of the man from Ghana. I wanted to call the police. I wanted to console the daughter. Did her rear end hurt? Her father had violated a code of ethics, but because he'd kicked her on the buttocks, an intimate zone, she couldn't stand neutrally apart from the violation and judge him. She would necessarily internalize the violation, as if the kick had emerged from *inside* her body, rather than outside. She was stained by his conduct, as we, watching, were also stained. The stain, contagious, hung like a cloud over California. We felt the stain in our bodies—as if the father had physically left a mark on us. And yet against my better judgment I felt a rueful, despairing pity for the father, who'd destroyed any possible future chance of happiness for himself and for his daughter, and who didn't seem aware that he had poisoned the future, like spilling oil into an ocean and never being able to clean it up. Just now, I wanted to write "clean up its incarnadine," because Shakespeare used the word "incarnadine" in such a circumstance, when it became time to describe eternal guilt, or a murderer's never-to-be-remediated hand. Shakespeare would have used the word "incarnadine" to describe the consequence of the father's act, but I've lost my chance. Let's say I've forfeited it. I've ruined my last chance for the rest of recorded time to use the word "incarnadine" unselfconsciously. The daughter would be stuck idealizing the father for years, and the idealization would occur, in her body, exactly at the spot where she had been humiliated; the sensation of *pain in the buttocks* would be twinned with the memory of *bystanders observing my kicked buttocks, bystanders observing my criminal father, bystanders observing my criminal misbehavior, bystanders unable to adjudicate, bystanders knowing that my family is rotten, bystanders being disgusted by the foulness of my flushed, tearful face.* If there is a caul surrounding us all, a caul of safety and mutual trust, a caul that constitutes us as civilized, then the father, with his violent yet enigmatic act, had torn that caul apart, and we all stood together in the drenching light, exposed to each other, exposed as helpless, as complicit, as voyeurs, as coparticipants in his crime. I imagined that the girl would feel queasy henceforth every time she looked at her father—queasy with the knowledge that he was attractive, and queasy with the knowledge that he had humiliated her, and queasy with the knowledge that in response to humiliation she wanted to murder him but lacked the power to act because in the exact place where she wanted to kill him she also loved him. At the risk of grandiosity, at the risk of acting in bad faith, I dedicate these fragments to the daughter whose father kicked her ass at the airport on Easter Sunday.

ACKNOWLEDGMENTS

Thank you to David Rogers, brilliant editor; to Ira Silverberg, beloved agent; to Sam Douglas, emboldening muse; to Bruce Hainley, Maggie Nelson, Lisa Rubinstein; to my literature students at the CUNY Graduate Center and my painting students at the Yale School of Art; to everyone at Picador; to my parents, my brothers, my sister; and to Steven Marchetti, magical beyond words.

PHOTOGRAPHIC PERMISSIONS

Quotations from Antonin Artaud, *Watchfiends & Rack Screams: Works from the Final Period,* edited and translated by Clayton Eshleman with Bernard Bador, used by permission of Exact Change publishers, Boston, 1995.

Jean-Michel Basquiat art permissions from © 2010 The Estate of Jean-Michel Basquiat/ADAGP, Paris/ARS, New York.

CPRKR © 2010 The Estate of Jean-Michel Basquiat/ADAGP, Paris/ARS, New York.

Television and Cruelty to Animals by Jean-Michel Basquiat, courtesy of © Christie's Images Limited 1998.

Eroica II, courtesy of Lio Malca Gallery and Christopher Burke Studio, New York.

James Castle's image, courtesy of James Castle Collection and Archive, Boise, Idaho.

Untitled (I Feel Most Colored When I Am Thrown Against a Sharp White Background) by Glenn Ligon, courtesy of the artist.

Untitled (I Am a Man) by Glenn Ligon, courtesy Regen Projects, Los Angeles, © Glenn Ligon.

Spell for Léon Fouks by Antonin Artaud, © 2011 Artists Rights Society (ARS), New York/ADAGP, Paris.